C000050978

One-Parent Families

One-Parent Families

A PRACTICAL GUIDE

SUE WATKINS

The Crowood Press

First published in 1989 by
The Crowood Press
Ramsbury, Marlborough
Wiltshire SN8 2HE

© Sue Watkins 1989

All rights reserved. No part of this publication may be
reproduced or transmitted in any form or by any means,
electronic or mechanical, including photocopy, recording
or any information storage and retrieval system, without
permission in writing from the publishers.

British Library Cataloguing in Publication Data

Watkins, Sue
    One-parent families: a practical guide.
    1. Great Britain. Single-parent families. Manuals
    I. Title
    362.8'2'0941

    ISBN 1 85223 177 7

Dedication
To Naomi, Thomas and Charlotte, with love

Typeset by Consort Art Graphics   Exeter   Devon
Printed in Great Britain by Billing & Sons Ltd., Worcester

Contents

Acknowledgements

The bulk of this book is based on twelve in-depth interviews with single parents. The interviews were sometimes very harrowing, because in describing what had happened to them people re-lived the events, sometimes for the first time in years. There were many occasions when both interviewer and interviewee were moved. I can only express my gratitude to those who did agree to be interviewed for their courage and co-operation in being so totally open and honest with me, sometimes at the expense of their own feelings. Perhaps unsurprisingly, all names in the book are fictitious. I should thank especially the non-custodial parents, the children and the teachers who were interviewed, and those teachers who completed questionnaires. Without their contribution the book would have been a very one-sided account. Also, I must express a big thank you to the many friends who have given me support and encouragement to undertake what at times seemed a very daunting task. I think we all heaved a sigh of relief when the book was finally completed. Last, but of course not least, thank you to my children for tolerating the tap of the typewriter in the living room and the many distractions which the book has created.

Introduction

So – you are on your own with the children. How will you cope? How will they cope? Are you a survivor, a fighter, or a victim? Being a lone parent today has lost much of the stigma that it carried with it in the past, but even traditional two-parent families face tremendous changes in society now. It can be pretty tough going if there is only one of you, *but* there are ways of managing, some compensations and eventually perhaps, a brighter future.

This book aims to describe the different experiences of single parents and to come to some conclusions about the best way of dealing with situations. It is primarily based on the opinions of twelve interviewees, and on those of the writer herself. The sample of subjects was a totally random one except in the balance of eight women and four men. They all bear the main, if not all the responsibility for their children. Some of them are friends of friends, others have been gathered from different Gingerbread groups. One or two were already well known to the writer, others known by sight, many were complete strangers. Despite this they do seem to represent a good cross-section of background and circumstance, but as is often stressed in the book, each and every case is absolutely unique.

Each case could have been presented as a story in itself, and in drawing together common experiences and trying to identify different courses of action I may not always have best represented what was said. Sometimes a quote has been used to demonstrate a point when perhaps if it was put in its original context the flavour of it would be a little different. If this has happened it is only because I believe the point to be generally representative. So, sincere apologies to anyone who feels that a quote is misplaced or over-stressed.

Whilst trying to represent everyone's views as honestly

as possible I have deliberately left out some of the most bitter comments because they are so unconstructive. Only one person I talked to was aggressively bitter, and one other sadly so. Bitterness, on the part of the sinned against, and guilt from those judged to have sinned, are the two most destructive reactions to what has happened. They should be guarded against at all costs. Whilst often justifiable, they are never permissible.

It was not within the ambit of this book to try to analyse *why* things went wrong with a marriage, but in order to set the scene I have described the causes as they were reported to me. The main objective was to find out how everybody reacted when they did go wrong, and how the custodial parent coped in the long run.

The process of separation is a lengthy one. It does not happen the day your partner leaves, or when you receive your decree absolute. The first two years after separation are full of trauma, and it may be several years before you have resumed what could be called a 'normal' existence. In the early days the most helpful philosophy is to take one day at a time – on very bad days one hour at a time! This book does not aim to save marriages (although for those thinking of separating it may well make them think again), but rather to enable those newly-separated to learn from other people's experiences and to make the best of their circumstances for themselves and their children.

1 The Bombshell

HOW IT HAPPENS

One thing very evident from my research is that every single relationship is unique. I shall try to draw comparisons and highlight similarities in order to gain as much benefit as possible from common experiences, but it must be remembered that the circumstances in every case were quite different. In any event, this section is obviously most useful as a source of information rather than practical guidance – virtually impossible to give on this point!

One factor that recurred in my findings, although I had not intended to research it, was a difference in background of the marriage partners. Although the reasons given for a separation were stated to be violence or infidelity, many people were basically disillusioned with their marriage partner after the 'honeymoon' was over. The end of the period of compatibility most commonly occurred with the birth of the first child. Up to this point people tended to make allowances for each other, enjoying the positive aspects of the relationship, and to a large extent turning a blind eye to differences in lifestyle.

The birth of the first child quite often triggered a jealousy reaction in the father, leading to arguments about how much money and time should be spent on the baby. More general principles about the rearing of the children would often be a cause of friction. In one extreme case where the parents disagreed on the child's upbringing the father became a muslim soon after the birth:

'He found birth and responsibility very hard to handle.
He rejected us. His way of coping was through religion
and I could not come to terms with the religion he
chose. I feel he chose that religion because it was male

dominated – it was his way of trying to gain control of us.'

In other cases aggravational behaviour tended to become more regular – drinking, smoking and gambling on the part of the men, leading to nagging and arguments from the women.

In several cases where men had been left by women for no specific reason I suspect that a basic incompatibility had become too hard to bear. The fact that the men could not understand why their wives had left underlines the lack of communication and understanding between them, totally unintentional and without malice on the part of the men. Sometimes this has happened over many years as the partners have changed and grown apart, but quite often there is a fundamental difference in outlook from the start, which should have been sorted out at an early stage. When talking to me people often referred to how their families handled situations and the different way that their partner's family behaved. One woman summed it up as follows:

'In particular I think people rush into marriage too quickly (I did myself), without a fair understanding of the other person's background and thinking about relationships. You have got to establish that your philosophies are the same before you have children, that your expectations are the same. In the past people living in small communities would have grown up together; their families would have had similar sorts of experiences; they would have known each other from birth. Whereas my parents were a devoted couple, his father had gone out drinking and had women friends. That was entirely outside my experience or the experience of anyone that we knew. My parents were always discussing and talking and he used to come home from work and not speak to me – perhaps for a whole weekend. He would come home, lie on the settee, put on the television and smoke. At first I didn't know what

12

I'd done and I used to cry. He's told the children
fairly recently that I was always crying. It's not their
experience that I'm always crying. I was so worn down
by it. There would be longer spells when he would not
speak to me – almost two weeks at a time. In the end I
got so sick that I walked out.'

SOME SITUATIONS LEADING TO FAMILY BREAKDOWN

Violence

Amongst the women violence was cited as the cause in two
cases. In both cases the violent partner came from a large
family – twelve and ten – and in one case was married at
seventeen. In this instance the marriage lasted twenty-two
years and saw the birth of six children. Until the birth of
the first child the husband was said to be 'golden'. From
then on, however, he admitted to feeling jealous of the
children. Although they never went short or wanted for
anything both wife and children lived in fear of the
husband's temper:

'He was bad when he'd had a drink, but he was worse
when he didn't. He'd knock me about, and the
children. They were frightened of him.'

In this case it was the eldest daughter who forced her
mother's hand after a bad attack of drinking and violence. Her mother had started proceedings in the past, but
had not felt strong enough to pursue them. This time her
daughter went with her to the solicitors, and the older
children supported her throughout.

In the other case the marriage lasted seven years and
saw the birth of two children. In this case the husband was
known to be a gambler but again things stayed in check
until the birth of the first child. The husband became
violent when he realized that a lot of money had to go on

13

baby things, and as time went on the family lived in fear and poverty. The husband vented his aggression on the wife and on possessions, but not on the children. This lady managed to maintain a stoic sense of humour about her situation. She described how on one occasion her husband had ripped the cooker from the wall and thrown it over his shoulder:

> 'I wouldn't have minded if it weren't for the fact that
> I'd just cleaned the bloody thing.'

In a third case the reason given for the breakdown was mental and physical abuse. Again the triggering factor seems to have been the birth of the first child, on which the partner suffered a nervous breakdown. He could not cope with the responsibility of the new baby and behaved in a bizarre way. The mother decided she had had enough when he started dismantling the electrical wiring, and she moved out to protect her own and her child's well-being.

In each of these cases the wives had been unhappy for a considerable time and made their decisions with some reluctance, but also with relief.

New Partners

New partners account for most of the other cases I researched. Again I must emphasise the individuality of every case, but inasmuch as one can generalise, three husbands were having a flippant affair or a series of affairs, three wives left to embark on new permanent relationships and one husband did the same.

In cases where one partner leaves in favour of another a common feature seems to be the timing or manner of the departure. In several cases the deserted party felt that their partner had either 'set them up' or timed their departure to coincide with a particularly vulnerable period, so that the deserted party was not in a position to fight back. In one case the wife was actually giving birth in hospital when her husband told her that he had installed a new partner in the matrimonial home. In another the husband was in prison, put there he feels, by his wife, whilst she moved a new partner into their home. In a third case a husband who worked night-shifts as a security guard felt duped by his boss, who controlled all his movements, and who disappeared with his wife and the proceeds from the business one night when he was on duty. In all these cases the helplessness of their situations at the time of separation has caused them bitter anguish to a greater or lesser degree.

In several of the cases overall there has been a separation in the past. In several cases psychiatric help or marriage guidance had been sought, but failed. In a number of cases one or other of the partners had suffered from depression or a nervous breakdown either before or after the separation.

PRECIPITATING FACTORS AND THE DAY OF SEPARATION

Most people remember vividly the actual day of separation. They know the day of the week it was and the exact times that things happened, even if years have elapsed since the event. In those cases where one partner had been unhappy for many months they usually remember a single event that was the proverbial straw that broke the camel's back. In one case it was the Friday that the husband came home from work having gambled away his week's wages. In another the Christmas Eve that the children were kept up to see their constantly absconding Dad who said he'd gone out to get crisps, but who did not return until long after they had gone to bed. In a third case it was the phone call from a woman that confirmed suspicions that an affair was taking place. In these and similar cases the women felt pushed past endurance to take action. They made a resolve there and then to bring the marriage to an end, and despite obstacles, difficulties and a few qualms, they remained single-minded in this resolve.

In most of the other cases a new partner was cited as the precipitating factor for the separation. Sometimes there had been problems already evident in the marriage, but in practically every one of these cases the deserted partner was still taken by surprise when the event happened. In the four cases where women left men, none of them discussed their decision with their husbands or children before acting on it. The shock, hurt and blow to their husbands' pride was the first and most lingering reaction. In all cases where spouses were taken by surprise on the day of separation they suffered varying degrees of mental breakdown.

The effect of the separation on practically all parties was traumatic. Despite the fact that people were quite willing and able to talk about their experiences, and in many cases have come to terms with their situations, found new partners, lifestyles or compensations, the underlying message that comes across from people who have suffered separation is that of coming through a tremendous ordeal. I mention this, which may seem obvious, only because there can be a tendency in society to feel that because something has become predominant or commonplace, it is less stressful than in the past. The formal machinery to structure such changes in society are very slow moving, and do not give much more support now than they have in the past. As we shall see, family and friends are the most important props to one parent families, and with the slow breakdown of the traditional family, friends become paramount.

THE HARDEST THING ABOUT THE ACTUAL SEPARATION?

There was quite a wide variation in replies to this question. For some who come from traditional close-knit families it was the fact that the family was broken up. Facing parents was sometimes hard, especially where one partner had lied or covered up for the other for months or even years. Accepting it themselves was hard in these cases, but knowing that they would be upsetting or hurting other family members made it harder.

In the cases where men had been left, their pride suffered a tremendous blow. As one man said:

> 'It's not knowing why, that is the hardest factor. My solicitor has got letters from her saying I've done nothing wrong – that I've been a good father, a good husband, nothing at all to fault me for. I still think at times that it must be something that I've done or something that I haven't done. Without a proper reason, to me its not a reason just to go.'

And again from another man:

> 'Pride. You can't justify why it came to that. The marriage was not perfect – I've not seen a marriage that was perfect – but I felt it had the foundations of being a good marriage. At least, I felt that I was doing the best I could, which was bloody good compared to whatever. To come to terms with the fact that that wasn't good enough – but not only that – she rejects your child as well, one hell of a thing to come to terms with.'

These men had been married for twenty-one and ten years respectively.

For some the worst thing was the fear of not being able to cope alone. One very capable and devoted mother whose children have grown into young adulthood quite successfully, described how in the very early days she would roll around on the floor banging her head in desperation. She was terrified that she would not be able to cope.

Women making the decision to go for a divorce some-times find the finality of the decision difficult to come to terms with. Sometimes they make several attempts before

they take the final steps and even then it's not straightforward. Jean described the hardest thing as the day her
husband was packing:

> 'In one way I wanted to say don't go. I still felt care
> for him despite how he'd been to me and the children –
> you can't wipe out twenty years just like that. But then
> in a way I was relieved when he'd gone.'

For a woman in married quarters of the RAF the worst
thing was having to get out of the accommodation straight
away. Despite the fact that this lady had felt desperate
enough about her marriage to take an overdose prior to
separation, she found it impossible to get local authority
assistance with housing if she left. This led her to become
reliant on the goodwill of a new partner to house her – not
really the best foundation for stability when she was
striving for independence.

SOME EARLY EFFECTS OF SEPARATION ON PARENTS

Practically everybody reported a sense of unreality about
what was happening, which lasted for weeks and often
months. People talked of being in a dream-world, of
expecting to wake up and find things different, of lack of
concentration and of viewing things from the outside.

For those people who have been abandoned, deserted
or deceived by their partners, separation obviously brings
a lot of heartache. Most commonly reported was a lack of
self-confidence, sense of inadequacy and inability to trust
others:

> 'Outwardly, I appeared to be in total control, inwardly
> devastated. It was worse at the beginning, and its still
> bad now. You survive. You become a little bit stronger, a
> bit more immune to it, but the feelings are still there.'

'No confidence. It's affected me at work – I've no confidence.'

'I was very hurt. That will never quite go away. It's different without children, you're not so vulnerable. I had to stop in with the kids.'

Very often, however, it was stated that without the children, the partner left would not have survived. On the other hand, there were also times when even the children did not seem enough to struggle on for.

Mental Breakdown

Some people suffer far greater mental instability as a result of separation than others. For some the worst effects hit them first, for others things get harder as time goes on. Three people I spoke to admitted having what they described as mental breakdowns. The most severe case occurred two months after his wife had left him and the four children. Peter described how he felt devastated to start with. He did what he had to to keep home and family going, but then cut himself off totally. He finally took an overdose and was admitted to a psychiatric hospital for six months. 'I'm not ashamed of it. They did me a power of good, they helped me a lot.' Peter was treated with counselling and groupwork, not drugs.

In the second case the man reported a total loss of confidence. He covered up all the mirrors in his home and could not cope with his job. Fortunately he sought help from his GP before things got too bad and was referred for counselling. At first he attended the hospital twice a week, decreasing this as time went on, until he didn't go at all:

'I went to the doctor. They sent me to the hospital, head cases, you know. I knew I'd got to look after my son. If it wasn't for him I don't know what would have

happened. The way I am – more emotional – that's how
it affected me. I lost about a month off work. They were
OK about it at work though, because I never used to lose
any time. I had a woman psychiatrist. She used to ask me
a lot of questions. She was OK. She talked to me. She
did not want me to have tablets if I could manage
without. At my last appointment she gave me her
number in case I ever needed it, but I never did.'

Both these men seem to have responded well to their
treatment.

In the third case the man was already in prison when he
learnt of his wife's desertion. He was treated for his
mental distress by being put in a padded cell in a straight-
jacket for three days. This man carries a tremendous
amount of anger and aggression about his situation and
says he learnt bitterness and hatred in prison.

If you are suffering mental stress beyond your endurance seek help from your doctor quickly. Ask to be
referred to a counsellor – many people seek help like this
at a later date and wish that they had done so sooner. Take
note of this advice from Peter:

'Don't try to cope on your own. Seek help – there's
plenty of help. Go to the doctor, or social services.
Don't try to fight it on your own. It nearly cost me my
life and the children their father. There's an awful lot
of people qualified to help. My experiences with helping
agencies have been nothing but good.'

(*See* Chapter 10 for other sources of help at this time.)

Drugs and Sleeping Tablets

No one can expect to come through a separation without a
degree of depression or sleeplessness – unless they are
Saints, Devils or Angels! How you cope with it will
obviously depend on your individual circumstances, and
quite importantly, how much support you get from

friends and family. Whilst it is important to seek help from your doctor if you need it, do be strong and ask to be referred to a counsellor to talk through your problems if that is what you feel you need. Several people who sought help from their GPs were prescribed tranquillisers or sleeping tablets. The consensus of opinion seems to be that they do not help. In one or two cases they were said to work when used for a short period – one prescription – and obviously if you are strung up and unable to relax anything is worth a try for immediate relief, but long-term you must find some other form of therapy to benefit you. Here are some people's reactions to using medication:

'I did ask for tranquillisers. They said I didn't need them. It was a natural reaction to stress. I tried them just to see if it would help me through some winter months, but I felt worse.'

'I was taking tranquillisers for fifteen months and in the end realised that they were doing me absolutely no good at all. It was pure addiction.'

'I did have palpitations when the troubles were bad. The GP prescribed tablets and made it clear that I could have some more if I wished. I only took a few. I knew this was not the sort of help I needed.'

'I am under the doctor for my nerves. That started before he left – gone five years. He gave me tablets. I don't want to get in the habit of using them, but if I feel like last night – shouting and upset – I took two tablets. They do calm me down. Some days I would prefer to have someone to talk to. You feel that you are just on your own.'

Talking to someone is generally the most constructive form of therapy. Women tend to have friends or relations emotionally closer to them than men. Men did find talking about things helped, but found it much harder to approach anyone to discuss things. They tended to respond better in a formal counselling setting (*see* Chapter 9 for other forms of therapy).

Food Fads

During the early months after separation people often reported lack of appetite. Several people lost a lot of weight. The general pattern seems to be a total loss of interest in food and inability to eat. Usually this caused more concern to those around the person suffering than the sufferer themselves. The person concerned usually felt that they eventually ate when they had to, or when there was a lull in the stress that they were feeling, and that after a period of time the problem resolved itself anyway.

Nevertheless, it did cause some people to lose weight dramatically, and in a couple of cases I suspect that they are still underfeeding themselves after many years, despite the fact that they are health conscious and very aware of nutritional needs. In some cases the problem extended to the feeding of the children, because the parent could not face preparing and cooking food. In these cases children usually enjoyed a period of convenience foods and easy snacks. If you are suffering an inability to face food the first message is not to worry about it. It is obviously stress-related and this can only exacerbate the situation. Eat small amounts as often as you can and provide the children with plenty of healthy snacks – milk, fruit, yoghurts, eggs and cheese. Beans on toast and fish and chips are both well-balanced meals which can be tolerated for some time by most children. Jacket potatoes are another good staple which need a minimum of preparation and can be varied by the addition of cold meat, tinned fish, salad or beans. If you are concerned about your child's diet because of your temporary abhorrence of food you could give them a daily multi-vitamin tablet as a precaution. Most children will not let their own food needs be ignored anyway! Obviously if the problem persists in a severe form for more than a couple of weeks you must seek medical help.

One or two people reported eating for comfort, or going on binges which they later regretted. Obviously over-eating or unhealthy eating is something to be guarded against. Activity is a good counteraction (*see also* Chapter 9).

Alcohol

Sleeplessness, loneliness, isolation or stress were given as reasons for people seeking consolation in drink. Women admitted to one or two wines or sherries after work or at bedtime. Men confessed to heavy lone drinking sessions late into the night. Home-made wine seems to be a danger-zone, being comparatively cheap and available in large supplies:

> 'When it first happened I'd drink. I just panicked. I used to make my own wine – I'd got a cellar-full of wine. I found I was drinking seven to eight bottles a night. I didn't go to bed. I'd sit in the chair.'

People enjoyed the anaesthetising effect of alcohol, although one woman reported that it made her mood worse and that it tended to make her aggressive. Several people had thought of contacting Alcoholics Anonymous, but all had brought their drinking under control without that help. If you suspect that your drinking is getting out of control bring it into check as soon as possible. Only allow yourself the use of a very small glass and only purchase drink in very small quantities. Try phoning a friend before having a drink – this may take away the urge altogether, or sit down and put your thoughts on paper whilst you have a tea or coffee. Your own thoughts can make fascinating reading at the time, and later, and it may help you to clear the haze in your head. If drink is becoming a problem don't keep any in the house. Give it away to a friend or ask them to safeguard it for you. If necessary contact Alcoholics Anonymous – they are only a phone-call away.

Smoking

Only one person admitted to smoking more heavily as a result of the separation:

> 'When he first left, for about three years I didn't like doing it and didn't inhale properly. Then I had a bad throat and decided that was it. I stopped with no problem. I think the need for the dependence had stopped.'

One of the men had only been separated for a short time when he found the inspiration actually to stop smoking:

> 'I packed up smoking when I met this other girl. She doesn't like smoking. So I thought, you've got to do something for yourself, so I just packed it up. Just packed up sixty a day.'

Smoking is a costly and unhealthy addiction. If you already smoke try at least to smoke no more than usual at this time of stress – it can only aggravate your financial situation and your health.

Slight Affairs

One person admitted to resorting to 'slight affairs' during the first twelve months of separation. Despite the tremendous emotional instability that most people experience at first, there is a danger of falling into a substitute relationship quite quickly. The evidence of those I spoke to indicates that these liaisons at such times are doomed to failure. However, that is not to say that they do not serve a valuable purpose in providing comfort and support at a difficult time. Unfortunately, it is not uncommon for one or other of the partners to feel used when such a relationship is brought to an end. It is not easy to guard one's emotions at this time, but do beware of rash affairs. They can be hard to extricate yourself from, or you may be badly hurt again.

EARLY REACTIONS OF THE CHILDREN

The reactions of the children in the early days of separation are inevitably many and varied, and often upsetting. In many cases they could not be recalled with any accuracy or detail, partly I feel because the adults themselves were suffering such emotional turmoil, but also I suspect because it remains distressing to recall for ever afterwards, and tends to be blocked out of one's conscious memory. As one man said, whose wife had disappeared without trace for eighteen months:

'They did miss their Mum. I couldn't really cope with it. I just shut off.'

There seems to be a consensus of opinion that below a certain age a child is too young to be affected by separation:

'People say that Ruth is a very well-balanced child, but I think we separated at a very good time [babyhood] because she was too young to know really. I think when they get to know the father then it must affect them more.'

Certainly the most worrying reactions came from older children, although, naturally, early experiences which cause a child long-term insecurity or anxiety have an adverse affect:

'Heather [4 years] became very neurotic and insecure. It didn't seem to affect Alan [18 months] so badly. It

25

seems to me that below a certain age they are too young to be affected, and I think Alan was.'

Most parents seem to feel that their very young children were protected against change by their immaturity and acceptance of what their life offers them. Parents who have been alone since their children were babies expressed a pleasure and confidence in the fact that because their children had never known any other state they had not had to suffer a change in life-style.

In cases where there had been arguments and violence the reaction of the children was one of relief. Mark, aged four, turned to his mum after the first few quiet days of separation, during which there had been no other reaction and said: 'Mummy, there aren't going to be any more fights and arguments are there?' Similarly Jane, aged fourteen, resumed sitting in the living room instead of staying in her bedroom all the time. She had hated the atmosphere and tension between her parents, and she felt happier and more relaxed after the separation.

In other cases children reacted with a mixture of grief, tearfulness and anger at first feeling deserted. Older children's first reaction is often to reject the parent whom they see as at fault, and this can be exacerbated if the deserted partner expresses bitterness and resentment. Sometimes children blame themselves for what has happened and they can become introverted and morose. I did not come across any cases of this in my research, but if your child does react in this way seek expert help quickly from a counsellor, through your doctor or the school, or from the nearest conciliation service. Children should not suffer the heartache of self-reproach for something which was in no way their fault.

Most people I spoke to tried to explain what was happening and sometimes this helped, sometimes it seemed to make things worse. Be as honest as possible with your children, they have long memories and to try and lessen the immediate hurt by lies or deception can lead to complicated repercussions when the truth is revealed.

Here are parts of an account of one child's reactions after his mother had left him at home in the care of his father, when he was just eight, and had made no contact with him for a year:

'In the first month his attitude was 'I don't care'.
Then he started to care and would ask me questions about her. 'Have you seen mum? Do you know where mum lives? Has she not phoned?' Then I'd hear him crying a couple of times. I tried to comfort him but he was heartbroken. That lasted for two to three months, with him putting on a brave face, and then he became acclimatised to it, he accepted it.'

Later on we shall see how this little boy was re-united with his mum and how quickly the bond was re-established between them.

CHANGES IN THE CHILDREN AFTER A PERIOD OF TIME

In general the reactions of the children get better with the passage of time. Of course if the situation continues to be unsettled, and it often does for some considerable time, there may be set-backs in their recovery. However, if friction between the separated parties continues over a long period the children can even adapt to this in time. Providing that they are not directly affected their tolerance of conflict increases, and the effects on them lessen.

In cases where there had been violence or tension between the parents the children inevitably became happier and more relaxed. Despite this one mother did find it hard to discipline her sons once that fear of violence from their father had gone, but she is working hard at being consistent, and draws some strength and assistance from her older children.

Younger children, especially boys, sometimes resent the absence of a man if the mother has problems, for example, mending bikes and playing ball games. Grandads, uncles and men friends should be used to the maximum. Easier said than done, but even if we lived in a non-sexist world, two sexes do exist, and its important for the children to relate to both of them as equally as possible, and in as many different situations as possible – not only when seeking assistance.

In two cases girls deprived of their fathers were drawn into undesirable liaisons very young. In both cases they had remained alientated from their own fathers for years. Girls seem less forgiving than boys, and sadly sometimes suffer from the lack of a second parent who would often welcome their association. On the other hand, younger children can sometimes be very open and affectionate with members of the opposite sex if they are missing that parent, and should be protected from getting too close to people inappropriately.

One man separated from his wife for eight years described another phenomenon very aptly by saying: 'my daughter's fourteen going on eighteen. She's grown up too quick.' Quite often the children are said to have old heads on their shoulders. It is sometimes difficult not to rely on one's children for help and support more than if there was a second parent around. Of course, it can do them a power of good to gain some independence and proficiency at household chores, but then one cannot be surprised if problems arise at a later date if father or mother wish to introduce a new partner to the household. In giving and expecting adult responsibility from our children we forfeit the right to decide and determine household matters without consulting them. Their approval will often not be forthcoming if and when they see someone approaching the camp to 'usurp' their position.

There were two cases where parents reported serious behavioural problems with their teenage children. In one case the parent was extremely bitter and angry about his situation. In the other the parent had suffered excessive insecurity and anxiety about her circumstances. In both cases I feel this had affected the children. This highlights the need to get your own emotions and situation sorted out as soon as possible. Don't neglect yourself or put yourself bottom of the pile. You are the main source of health and well-being for your children, so it is not selfish to ensure that you are in a strong position to provide these.

2 Going Public

EARLY DAYS

The structure of the family today is complex. It varies considerably from one family to another and from one community to another. Background, life experiences, financial and practical considerations all influence the way we organise and run our families. The early days of single parenthood are often the time when a lot of support is needed, but not always sought because of the embarrassment of the situation and the strong emotions often attendant at that time. The repercussions within families of a separation tend to spread much further than people anticipate, and last for months and often years after.

RELATIONS WITH RELATIONS

What will other people think of your situation and does it matter? The people I spoke to tended to fall into one of two categories. Either they were not too worried by other people's reactions, or else they were all consumed by self-consciousness over what had happened.

Those not too worried by what others thought generally came from families where everyone already seemed to know the situation, even if nobody had acknowledged it. Often in these cases the parents were the first to express relief and to reassure the newly-estranged partner that they had done the right thing:

'Well, I wasn't particularly worried about my family because I expected them to be supportive about it.'

'I wasn't worried because my parents knew I was

30

doing the right thing and all my neighbours knew what
he was like.'

None the less, parents can often wish you out of a bad
situation without necessarily having the means or incli-
nation to help you with the resultant chaos.

'I realised just how much my parents influenced me
and, in a way, wanted me to break away, but were not
particularly understanding of my situation.'

Even when your relatives are relieved that you have taken
a decision, and, at times, are forthcoming with practical
help and support, there will still be many other times when
you feel alone with no one to turn to. Each new situation
that arises demands energy and resourcefulness from you
to deal with it. Draw strength from the fact that you are
not the only one in your situation. Many others have been
there before you and come through it eventually (*see*
Chapter 10 – 'Gingerbread').
People who were really worried by what their families or
parents would say had often spent much of their married
lives covering up the real situation, and found it hard to
face up to the shock or surprise of revealing the truth:

'To a lot of people we had a super marriage. A lot of
people were devastated, incredulous at what the
relationship was really like.'

'Everyone said how well-suited we were. People at
school didn't realise that when he collected the kids
from school it was because I'd got a black eye – they
thought how good he was.'

'It took me four years to tell my father. He really liked
my wife. He thought she was lovely. I used to make
excuses – she's busy, she's not well – that sort of stuff.
My sister told him in the end.'

31

Talk to people and tell people as much as possible. It might help you sort things out in your own mind. Write out your thoughts for yourself if necessary. People can only be shocked or sorry once – the initial reaction is usually the worst to bear, after that its a matter of getting on with life. Sadly the next week it will be someone else's turn to be hit by the 'bombshell', and your troubles will fade into insignificance.

Sometimes you may find yourself comforting relatives or friends when what you needed was a shoulder to cry on. Try to be strong, honest and open at times like this. Honesty from the start with those close to you – relatives, friends and neighbours – pays dividends in the long run. It may mean admitting that you do not like what you have done, but you felt you had to do it. If people choose to judge you or react to what you tell them there is very little you can do about it. They will judge you in private anyway, so nothing is gained from trying to hide the facts, except that you may then load yourself with extra guilt at a time when you need your energy for more constructive activities such as caring for the children and meeting their needs.

REACTIONS FROM PARENTS/FRIENDS/NEIGHBOURS

Incredulity

It can be difficult for people outside a marriage to understand that what appeared to them to be a perfectly satisfactory relationship in fact had many flaws, incompatibilities and hidden unhappiness. It can be hard, too, to realise that a much-loved son/daughter or 'in-law' who has many worthy and positive attributes could actually do something as dramatic as end a marriage, causing apparently needless hurt to those nearest and dearest to them:

'My husband did a lot of things for my parents. They thought he was wonderful. They could not believe it at first.'

No one other than the two partners concerned can really understand what brings a relationship to an end – and the real reasons may elude even them. Once the decision has been made to part company very little can be gained from trying to justify or apportion blame for what has happened. Those people coping best with their separation seemed to take the attitude that although they did not like what had happened they had to look to the future and think positively.

Rejection

After the initial shock of what has happened do your best to keep all channels of communication open. Sometimes one partner is rejected by family and friends. Whatever has happened between you, your children will always have two parents, and if they maintain a healthy contact with both, this increases their chances of keeping in touch with grandparents, aunts and cousins. This can be more and more important as time goes on. The use of the conciliation services can be invaluable at this critical time if you feel that you are losing control of healthy communication.

Gossip

During the early days you may find you are the talk of the neighbourhood. It is important for you and the children that you get out and about, facing the neighbours and talking about topics other than your separation as soon as possible. Do not feel that you have to give a complete background story to every person who hits upon the subject of your new status. Sometimes it may seem as if everyone was in the know but you:

33

'One neighbour said: "I could have told you she was playing about".'

'The neighbours already knew from the shouting and screaming. I didn't need to say anything.'

'I told the neighbour and she said: "About bloody time".'

However, whatever it appears, neighbours do not always know everything. They only know what is evident, and they sometimes misjudge from that.

'Their reaction was that he had been rotten, and they called him everything to my face. At the same time they could not understand how I covered up so much, because we always looked happy. Although they were nice to your face you knew they were talking behind your back.'

Close your ears to things you do not want to hear and only say as much as you want to. State your case clearly if you have to, but do not be lured into lengthy explanations. The immediate crisis will soon pass and they will get used to your new status. Do not get the reactions of neighbours out of proportion:

'To me it didn't matter what they thought. They knew what I was like, and as long as they didn't think any the worse of me, it didn't matter to me.'

Support

Friends in particular often rally round at times like this. Accept help gracefully whenever possible, but try to keep the lives of the children as near as possible to their normal routine. It can be helpful to pour out each incident as it occurs to close friends, but do not fall into the trap of becoming the current entertainment. Always try to take an interest in the health and well-being of those you are chatting to so that your sessions do not become a one-way affair, where you almost feel a failure if you cannot provide some recent snippet of marital antagonism. Try also to reserve your most emotional sessions for when the children are in bed. Obviously the children will know what's happening and should never be expected to keep the situation secret, but its not healthy for them to be witnesses to regular lengthy sessions when they hear only one side of the story. It can make it difficult for them to retain loyalty to both sides, and cause a loss of respect for the divulging party.

CONTACT WITH PARENTS AND IN-LAWS

Try to maintain the same contact as before with your parents and your in-laws. Sometimes your feelings of anger, resentment or shame may extend to the parents of your partner. You may feel that the very fact they are related means that they will condone your partner's behaviour and condemn yours. Evidence is quite the contrary. Parents do tend to keep in touch with their own son/daughter, whoever they see as at fault, but they do not always agree with their behaviour. The most important thing as far as they are concerned is that the children are not deprived of a set of grandparents. If you find it difficult to face your in-laws at first, try dropping them a line stating simply that you regret what has happened, but hope that they will still wish to see the children. As they get older the children can visit them without you. As well as being important for them it can give you a welcome break.

Some people I spoke to were able to maintain fairly close and regular contact with their in-laws despite the rift, and some in-laws chose to support their own child's spouse and to cease contact with their son/daughter. As events proceed sometimes things happen in court or actions are taken by solicitors which cause fresh stresses and strains.

Try not to let this affect your wider relationships. Always remember that they are not responsible for what has happened and it is in the interests of the children to continue to associate with them. Sometimes it happens that having lost their partner, people enjoy a sort of reunion with other family members, and this can be a bonus for them and the children.

CARING FOR THE CHILDREN IN THE EARLY DAYS

Unless the circumstances of your separation are such that you and your partner are able to share the care of the children between you, you will need to rely on someone else some of the time. It depends on the age of the children, but people often find it hard to part company with their offspring during the early days. It is a sort of 'clinging together' reaction. Follow your instincts about allowing other people to have the children during this period. If they are unusually tearful and clingy its probably best to stay with them, in the company of whoever. That way you have got someone with you to provide some company and break up what can be monotony and isolation. If the 'company' also has children of a similar age to yours they can benefit from normal play activities and this can give you a break.

If Your Children Are Under School Age

Get out and about as much as possible during the day. Go to as many usual places as you can – park, playgroups, mother and toddler clubs. You may feel that you have a large label on you saying 'lone parent' but in fact you look the same as usual to everyone else, and there is no need to broach the subject of your circumstances unless you want to. Think of a short phrase or potted version of what has happened, something which does not invite further questions if you do not want them, and then move on quickly to something else. Direct questions to whoever you are with usually stop 'incoming' queries!

It is unusal to find young children in the care of their father, but it does happen and probably will be increasingly so in the future. You will have to be fairly strong to avoid the sympathy brigade. It is not good for you or the children to be surrounded by women expressing sadness at your situation. You are probably sad about it too, but you have to be positive to survive. Try to say something simple but inoffensive that will stem the flow of sympathy and enable you to move on to actually enjoying the children and the company. Try to take an interest in other people and their children, but include and involve yours as well.

People I spoke to with babies or very young children relied heavily on their own parents for help and support at this time. Grandparents naturally enjoy a lot of contact with their grandchildren, but once that contact is such that it is no longer informal visits at each other's convenience, but rather essential support which cannot be withdrawn, it can lead to complications of its own:

> 'My parents gave me a lot of support. They would have Anna at weekends and help me out, but it was almost as if . . . my mother would say "we've brought Anna up".'

This parent felt that the emphasis of conflict shifted from her ex-partner to her mother. Before she had been worried by her partner's need to dominate her and the baby. Now she worried about the influence that her mother was having on the child's upbringing. This was because the help her mother offered was so important to her that she was dependent on it rather than choosing it.

Another mother who relied on her parents to care for three small children whilst she was out at her cleaning job, found she was reprimanded like a schoolchild if she was five minutes late coming home. Caring for small children is a strain on anybody, and when grandparents are asked to do it 'second time around' their patience and understanding is not always as elastic as it was in the past. Try not to be too narrow-minded yourself in your acceptance of your parents' help. It will probably only be intense for a temporary period – do your best to make it so – and the damage to young minds of well-meaning if misguided grandparents will be minimal compared to other fates that could befall them.

LONGER TERM HELP AND SUPPORT IN CARE OF UNDER-FIVES

Parent/Toddler Groups

These are more commonly known as mother/toddler groups, but please, fathers, be brave and introduce yourself! For parents with babies or toddlers they provide a useful change of scene. If you have not used one before, now is the time to seek one out. You will find one by asking at your local clinic, Citizens' Advice Bureau, social services or library. They usually meet one morning or afternoon a week and it will provide a time each week when you can look forward to being in the company of other people. They vary considerably, so if the first one seems full of fractious babies and broken toys, try another one. They vary also from week to week, according to who has turned up and how much sleep the parents have collectively had the previous night. So do not judge too quickly – try two weeks running just to check. When you get there talk to others, ask them about themselves and their children – that usually gets them chatting, and you will probably be able to buy yourself a welcome cup of tea – made and washed up by someone else. Bliss! Take as much benefit as you can from this break in what can be a lonely existence. A small word of warning though – you will still have to supervise your child as squabbles soon break out at this age. Try not to be offended if they do happen. They are soon forgotten if you allow them to be. Finally, when you have been attending for a few weeks ask if there is a rota for tea-making, there usually is, and whilst you should enjoy the weeks that it is not your turn, your offer of help will probably be gladly received.

Playgroups

These are for three to five year olds to attend, usually without their parent, although sometimes parents help in rotation, and if your child is clingy or upset you will usually be allowed to stay with them. If your child is this age s/he will benefit from associating with other children, learning to be sociable, and being independent of you for short spells. Playgroups have to be registered with the social services who supervise them and ensure that minimum standards are maintained. The toys and equipment will usually be things that you could not afford in your own home – slides, sand and water trays, bikes and other mobiles – so there is plenty to attract your child. Again you can find out where your local ones are by asking at the clinic, Citizens' Advice Bureau or social services. There is usually a small charge and children attend for varying numbers of morning/afternoon sessions – most commonly two or three. If you explain your circumstances you may get a place quicker.

Nursery Schools/Classes

Nursery classes are part of our education system, and are a good introduction to school routine for three and four year olds. They have a qualified teacher in charge, assisted by one or more nursery nurses. Provision varies considerably throughout the country, but places are usually hard to come by unless you get your child's name down when they are a baby. However, approach the headteacher or

39

teacher of your local nursery unit and explain your position and your child may be given some priority. Do not be put off if you have to go on a waiting list – people move house or drop out for other reasons and you will sometimes get a place quicker than expected.

Childminders

Generally unqualified, childminders tend to be experienced mothers who look after other people's children in their own home. They must be registered with the local authority, who visit and supervise them. The best place to find one is by asking at the local social services who may sometimes be able to suggest particularly appropriate people. Some childminders will take your child on an occasional basis, and providing your child knows the childminder well enough and likes going there, this can provide you with an invaluable break or opportunity to do something on your own. However, the majority prefer to have a child on a permanent, or at least regular, basis, as not only does this make it easier to care for the child, but it also forms a part of their regular income. Charges vary, but it is important to know what they are from the outset, together with any other conditions such as who pays for meals and outings. Childminders who come by recommendation or by personal friendship can work well. It is obviously much easier if the child already knows the person, but it is even more important to sort out the business side first. This will avoid misunderstandings which might otherwise cause more disturbance for your child. Similarly, if you are using a friend to care for your child and paying her to do so, you must place your complete trust in her to look after the child as she judges best during the time she has responsibility. This is not always an easy bridge to cross, and if you have doubts about it, it may be better to use a different person rather than risk losing a friend.

Day Nurseries

Day nurseries are listed in your local yellow pages and provide full-time day care for under-fives, including babies. At one time they were predominantly run by local authorities to help families with special needs. Nowadays they tend to be privately run and are primarily used by working parents. If you feel that you must get back to work for reasons of finance, health or sanity, day nurseries can provide the answer. Obviously you should thoroughly vet the day nursery of your choice to ensure that it is run along lines of which you approve. The cost of this sort of care can be quite high and each nursery has its own policy regarding admission and fees, but if it is the sort of support that you need it will be worth it.

Combined with help from family and friends, the use of any of the above can give you relief from the tremendous strain of coping with little ones twenty-four hours a day single-handed. If you feel that you are not coping well with your children at this time of stress do tell someone. Go to the local clinic and ask to see the health visitor, or phone the social services and ask for an urgent visit. There is a social worker on duty twenty-four hours a day, so if you find yourself under pressure out of office hours there will always be somebody available to give you help and advice. Ask directory enquiries for the number of the 'out-of-hours' social worker. Alternatively ring the Samaritans. Some areas have a Parents' Helpline for times like this. Ask directory enquiries, or look in your local directory in the community pages. Citizens' Advice Bureaux should have the number, but it's best to make a note of it when you are not at crisis point, and keep it by the phone. 'Gingerbread' often provide this sort of support to their members (*see also* page 159).

If you do approach social services for help, make sure you get the right offices to begin with. Many people get confused between the Departments of Health and Social

Security, which is where your benefits and allowances can be sorted out, and the local authority Department of Social Services, which is where social workers operate from, and where you should go to see one. A social worker should be able to give you general help and advice on how to get through this period, and if you are having problems with the children there are an increasing number of family service units to which you could be referred.

Family Service Units

These units provide all the facilities of day nurseries, and often of nursery classes, but encourage the involvement of the parents so that parents and children can spend time together in an unpressurised environment. It is also somewhere neutral where your partner could arrange to see the child if necessary. The staff have a variety of social work and child-care qualifications, and the officer-in-charge can also invite specialist staff such as child psychiatrists, speech therapists or audiologists as required. You are usually able to leave your child there to enable you to work, but you will also be encouraged to spend some time at the unit, involving yourself with your child as well as with other parents and possibly activities such as yoga. These units do not confine themselves to helping very young children, but aim to help the whole family and may well have activities for older brothers and sisters. You will be asked to make some financial contribution according to your means.

SCHOOL AGE CHILDREN

If your children are of school age, try to keep their daily routine as close as possible to how it has always been, except where that accentuates the 'hole' left by your partner. You may still have to rely on relatives or friends to help, but at least there is a part of every school day when you know that they will be safely occupied.

Those with older teenage children have often found them to be a great help at this time, looking after smaller ones after school and giving their parent support and companionship. Bear in mind though the danger of making them too grown-up, and do not confide your innermost feelings to them when you are vulnerable. Remember that they may be feeling mixed up too, and might find it hard to cope with your deepest anxieties – save these to share with other adults or the experts. Neither should you lean on them any more than you really have to for help with the little ones – it is not their fault that you are a parent alone, and they may come to resent you if you take advantage of them.

Similarly, if you get a lot of child-care support from your own parents or in-laws, that does not necessarily also mean that they can give you a lot of emotional support. Turn to friends or other helping agencies. It can some-times be tempting to discuss problems in the children's behaviour with your own parents. They may be able to put things in perspective or give you another point of view, but if you find that they are too closely involved and unable to be objective you might find it more helpful to have a chat with their teacher. They deal with children all day every-day and can often put your mind at rest.

3   Schools and Teachers

How, what and when should one speak to the teacher? Like doctors, teachers are daily presented with problems symptomatic of our age. So much so that you may find it hard to bring your child's teacher face to face with the reality that the child is facing a difficult period. Traditional qualities of modesty, discretion and embarrassment can sometimes lead teachers to make sweeping generalisations, such as separation being so commonplace, just to reassure you that they are not going to be judgemental. On the other hand, it would be an insensitive teacher indeed, who did not recognise the stress put on a child by separation, and there may be some who lay emphasis on this, compounding any guilt that you may already feel. A good third of a child's life is spent at school, and although in many ways this is somewhere that the child can escape from the changes in the rest of his world, it is probably best to inform the school sooner rather than later about changes in the pattern of his home life.

Every age has its particular problems, and every child is an individual, but often one of the obstacles to a child coming to terms with his parents' change of status is the reaction of other people. Even the youngest of school children need the approval of their teachers and peers. Avoidance of the issues can lead to in-built stresses and in behaviour designed to cover up what is happening.

TELLING THE PRIMARY SCHOOL

People I spoke to with primary age children told the school what had happened fairly soon after the event:

44

'As soon as I was capable – about two days afterwards. Its important for the teachers because of the effects on the children. Its surprising how helpful they can be.'

'The first time they went to school after it happened, just in case there was a reaction. Katy was a bit quiet so I said they could ring me to fetch her back if necessary. After that I talked to the teachers day by day.'

You can expect to become emotional at times like this. The first time of telling is always the worst, so go armed with tissues, and set aside time afterwards to have a cup of tea. It is not a pleasant duty, but it is a responsibility you have to bear for the sake of the children – much the same as having to hold their hand when they receive dental or medical treatment. It makes it much better in the long run.

It may be best to talk to the headteacher in the first instance. He will inform only those whom you wish to know, in a discreet manner. Personally I think it makes it easier all round if all staff know, including dinner ladies and playground staff. They all come into contact with your child and they may make insensitive remarks if they are not in possession of the facts. This does depend to some extent on the size of school, and the level of professionalism amongst the staff. After the initial information it is probably most appropriate to mention any further developments to the class teacher.

You should not tell teachers anything that you do not want to, only as much as you need to, and there is no way that you can keep them informed of every subtle shift of mood and circumstance that you are bound to experience. Nevertheless, news travels fast, and gossip and rumour faster still, so it is best to be direct and put the record straight from the start. Bear in mind all the time that the teacher's concern is your child. Of course, all this good basic groundwork will be completely wasted if the child is made to feel that the subject is taboo. Children find it harder than adults to keep secrets. They often need to confide in their friends. Their sense of disloyalty, failure and unhappiness if they let out some forbidden tit-bit of information can begin an escalation of insecurity.

It is best to arm the children with a phrase that fits the circumstances. Tell them their teacher will know and that if the children ask, they can tell them. Mostly, children will not ask, but having permission to tell is a good safety-valve for the child. It prevents worry building up inside about what they would do in the circumstances. It will depend on how unhappy or insecure they are feeling as to how well they handle the situation, and there is no doubt that children do hide a lot from their classmates. Secrets tend to be divulged in corners of the playground or sometimes on visits to the washrooms.

Whilst the news is still fresh it may be given this sort of treatment but after a time classmates soon recognise and accept what has happened.

TELLING THE SECONDARY SCHOOL

At this age telling teachers and classmates is a slightly different ball-game. Older children can cope better with keeping their home life separate from their school life, and apart from the friends of their choice with whom they associate, often do. Use your discretion whether or not you should formally notify the school. Obviously if the child is very different from normal something has to be said, but you should avoid upsetting the child even more if s/he is adamant that they prefer it not to be disclosed. If you are in a position to allow the child a day or two off school in the first instance, it may just give him a breathing space to prepare himself for facing others. What people think can be very important at this age, and if the child himself has not worked out how he feels about things it can be difficult for him to handle the reactions of his contemporaries. Discuss the matter as frankly as possible with the child –

what he can face up to and at what stage – but guide him into honesty as the best policy.

If the child is not too visibly affected, and would prefer you not to speak to teachers, it may be better that way:

> 'I discussed it with Jane. She wanted as few people as possible to know. There was a teachers' dispute at the time so there were no parents' evenings. I watched her reports carefully to see if there was any indication of effect.'

At a later date this parent was discussing options with the year tutor and took the opportunity to raise the subject. The teacher expressed surprise at what had happened and said that Jane was happy and well-balanced and that no disturbance had been reflected in her school work. In fact this separation had been quite turbulent at times, but with careful monitoring and observation of Jane's wishes, she came through it all right.

In other cases though, where parents themselves had been too upset by what had happened to cope with approaching the school, the children's work and behaviour had been affected. In two cases fathers were advised by some other agency to inform the school, and both times the school reported relief to find the cause of uncharacteristic behaviour. Experienced teachers might suspect some trouble at home in instances such as these, but it makes their job, and the child's life, a lot easier if they are informed in the first place.

> 'When I went up they said they were glad I'd come up; they could understand a bit more now. Andrew had been a bit funny, but at least they would know what was causing it. When I went up again after a few weeks they said he'd been a lot better, now they knew what was happening. When he moved to the other school, I had a word with them straight away.'

The majority of people I spoke to felt that teachers had handled the situation well, and that nothing more could have been done to improve matters. Primary teachers in particular were reported to be watchful, attentive and caring:

'Amy's teacher was very motherly and gave her plenty
of affection.'

In only one case did anyone feel that a teacher had behaved insensitively by making a child aged six stand up in class and asking him what his father's job was. As the child had never known his father he replied that he had not got a father, and was very upset by the incident. In two other cases parents were not happy with the way that teachers related to them as parents:

'The secondary schools don't involve you. They don't
treat you as a participant. Things I feel I ought to have
been told I found out subsequently.'

'I think they thought I was a bit of a rebel, a bit of a
problem. I get the feeling that they definitely think that
single parents are at a disadvantage.'

In the latter case, however, the parent still thought that the teachers handled her child well. Interestingly both these parents are trained teachers, and it may be that this is more significant than the fact that they are single parents.

INCIDENTS OR REMARKS AT SCHOOL

Occasionally an incident or remark from other children at school causes an upset. The absense of one parent seems to be the handle on which most of these remarks are hung. If your partner has been off the scene for some time when your child goes to school, ensure that they understand that they do have two parents, but that one is elsewhere. This simple precaution seems to satisfy them and their friends.

Its a good idea to welcome your child's schoolfriends into the house from the start. With young children it is up to you to make a point of inviting other children in to play. Not only will it distract your own children from dwelling on recent events, but it also helps to keep them integrated at school. You can expect the occasional remark in the early days, but again, be prepared with a simple but honest phrase describing the situation. 'John's dad lives somewhere else' or something along those lines covers most situations. Keep your ears open without being too obvious about it, and jump in with the phrase for your child if necessary. When you've said it on one or two occasions your child will see that it satisfies and will follow suit on future occasions:

> 'Yes, they sometimes ask why Mark's dad doesn't live here. I explain that he lives somewhere else and that's usually enough.'

You will not always be in a position to shield your child from the curiosity of others, but if you are able to deal with queries in an unemotional, matter of fact way, it will give him confidence to handle similar situations when you are not there.

Secondary age children may find it harder to face up to their contemporaries in the early days, but will usually confide in their close friends, and often draw a lot of support from them. Once the information is well known it usually ceases to be a problem, but until then it can be a source of great embarrassment:

> 'Liz [14 years] was upset by information of the divorce being passed round. She was very embarrassed by it. It didn't bother me because I could argue, I was sure of my ground, but Liz was not mature enough to deal with gossip. I tried to be as open as possible with her to give her support. It helped when it became apparent that one or two at school had divorced parents.'

Quite often the discovery that someone else is in the same boat takes a lot of the sting out of the situation, especially if that person is someone who is otherwise quite normal with no obvious symptoms for anyone to see. It can help your child to appreciate that life goes on, and that they are not suddenly different from the rest of the world. That is a good point to make to them if there are problems. At school nothing need be different from before. They will not be conspicuous unless they make themselves so by a change of behaviour. Then again, do not push this point too far too soon. In the very early days they may well need a period of introspection to recover emotionally.

SCHOOL FUNCTIONS

Attending school functions as a single parent can be a lonely and upsetting time, even though there may be other parents on their own. How you cope will depend on your own state of mind:

> 'There was no change really. I always went anyway, whereas the wife only went sometimes. But it felt really strange at first. It was more me knowing that I was on my own than other people.'

In some cases nothing changes on these occasions – partners never attended functions anyway. In others things improve because the partner who is now absent used to cause embarrassment:

> 'I think I felt better in a way. There was one incident when Jack first started school when my husband came with me. He really showed me up. I felt "Oh God, I wish I could just disappear". So on my own I could go up feeling relaxed.'

In most cases however, there is a certain amount of discomfort and self-consciousness, at least on the first few occasions.

Parents' Evenings

It will depend on how the parent evenings at your child's school are organised as to how difficult you might find this situation. In cases where there is an appointment system which is kept to, and parents go in to see the teacher individually it can be fairly straightforward. Aim to arrive promptly so that you are not waiting around musing for too long. If your lonesomeness does bother you, bear in mind that most parents have to come on their own anyway – leaving their partners in charge of the children. There will be other parents attending on their own for similar reasons to yours.

When it is your turn to speak to the teacher only bring up the things that cause you concern. If you have been a single parent for some time that obviously need not be mentioned unless there is a related problem. Newly separated parents may feel embarrassed on the first occasions. Try to be as objective as possible about the whole exercise. Your circumstances may be of some significance at this stage, but don't let that blind you to everything else. Take a keen interest in your child's work, methods of teaching and school policies in general. On the other hand, do not become too offensive. Some parents react to their own self-consciousness by criticising the school, other children or the teachers. This will help nobody and may make it harder for you to approach the staff at other times when you need their co-operation. Aim to work as a partnership with the teachers. Be open and honest about any worries you may have, but do not treat the occasion as a session in the confessional.

This applies even more in those cases where parents and teachers get together en masse in a classroom or hall. On these occasions you will be very aware that there are eyes and ears everywhere. Obviously you would like to be treated as similarly as possible to other parents, so if there is nothing strictly confidential that you need to discuss you will probably want to attend with everyone else. If what you have to say is not for public consumption most schools will accommodate you in private at another time. Primary schools in particular can be very helpful because you are on the premises so often anyway. If you find it hard to get a sitter to allow you out at night they will often see you just after school, allowing your child to browse in the library or play in the playground in good weather. Never miss a parents' evening because of embarrassment. These times are vitally important and an opportunity to discuss your child with another interested adult which you may well be missing at this time. As time goes by, you will find these occasions easier:

> 'At first it was awful. Watching other couples study work and smile at it, sharing it. It's all right now. I'm used to it. Everyone knows my circumstances and understands.'

Not every separation is acrimonious and in cases where the split has been, or has become civilised or even amicable, it is beneficial to keep your ex-partner informed of school progress. It will depend on the exact arrangements you have for the care of your child, but if your partner sees a lot of them, encourage them to take a turn at parents' evenings. Obviously you have to be on quite good speaking terms for this to work, as there is no point in the teacher saying things to one parent unless they are later to be shared with the other. Everyone benefits from everyone else knowing all that has been said. If it is not practically possible for ex-partners to attend parents' evenings, at least inform them when they take place, and give a précis of what was said. Write them a note if you do not have the chance to chat. The more information you feed to absent partners the easier they find it to keep in touch with the children, and the better that is for everyone.

Concerts and Sports Days

Concerts and sports days should be happy occasions when you can be proud of your children. It may be that at first these times cause you some discomfort because of the absence of your partner, and through lack of someone to turn to and share the little incidents that make these occasions. The best way to overcome this is to invite someone to attend with you. Grandparents are ideal, but if not, friends are almost as good. You will enjoy these functions far more by having someone to share them with. Do not try to face these things alone. Your mood and determination will show through on your face and will affect your child. Invite a friend, go with pride, smile at your child and inspire them with confidence.

Where your ex-partner is closely involved decide between you who should go to what. Quite often primary concerts are repeated so that you can go on different occasions. This is probably what most married parents will do anyway, so it keeps your child within normal conventions. Unless you get on really well and are able to sit together without embarrassment it is not the best plan for both parents to attend at once. It is confusing and can be distressing for a young child in particular to have to search the audience twice for that familiar face. It can also create worries of allegiance and loyalty which are best avoided.

Sometimes an embarrassing situation can arise and this is when you might appreciate co-operation from the staff. One mother described how she recently attended her son's sports day. Towards the end of the programme there was a fathers' obstacle race. Her son's father had been absent from their lives for about four years, and not wanting him to feel left out she readily volunteered to join in the race. Most of the other mothers were aware of her circumstances, but another dad, not so regularly at the school raised an objection to her taking part. In this instance a teacher diplomatically stepped in and explained, minimising if not totally alleviating any embarrassment.

In another case a father who, until then, had never attended any school functions, suddenly started turning up at every opportunity. Again the staff were able to keep an eye on the situation, and ensure that the child was safely delivered to the appropriate parent after school functions. Parents deprived of normal opportunities to see their children can be driven to desperate measures. Try your best to sort out arrangements for access as early and as amicably as possible.

AT THE SCHOOL GATE

Some people find it very hard 'at the school gate'. There is normally some point where parents tend to gather whilst waiting for their children to go in and come out of school. It may be in the playground, or on the pavement by the gates, but wherever, it tends to be a little community of its own, with its own methods of communication and inter-action. Not everybody enjoys this sort of fraternisation anyway, when the only thing you have in common is your reason for being there:

> 'I felt isolated and different from them at the school
> gate. I've stood at the school gate, but I've always
> stood alone.'

It can be harder still when you are first separated to face up to those who seem almost to live 'at the school gate'.

Surprisingly, those most lacking in confidence, who had suffered most in other senses, seemed somehow to be protected in this situation. They claimed it did not worry them what others thought, and more commonly, that they drew strength from knowing that they were not alone in their situation:

> 'I thought to myself, well I'm not on my own here. If I
> were to worry about what he or she thinks – well, they

54

might be in the same situation. It did worry me, but I overcame it.'

These people tended to be pleased and touched if offered sympathy. Other people, notably the normally confident, seemed to be more intimidated by the crowd in this situation:

'I felt self-conscious. I never heard anything said, but I saw heads turn and felt they were gossiping about me.'

'They reacted with sympathy. I look on that as a means of trying to find out sordid details.'

Both these people found it quite an effort to break through what seemed to them a psychological barrier to joining the group:

'They seemed to avoid me for a few weeks. I felt self-conscious. I took my courage in my hands and approached a group of mums. It was OK after that.'

'Initially I found it hard collecting him from school. Schools tend to be a clique, a community, and people can be quite cold to anyone different. You have to force yourself on someone. Once you've got that one person hopefully they are your avenue to communicate.'

If you find it a problem at the school gate do try to chat to someone. You will find that once you have broken through that invisible barrier things are much easier. Try to aknowledge people even if you don't want to chat, but do not be over sensitive if they appear to overlook you – other people have problems too and they may be pre-occupied with these.

A WORD FROM THE TEACHERS

In researching the views and opinions of teachers I only had the opportunity to interview two teachers. One of these interviews I have included verbatim because there are many helpful hints in it and it may be of interest to those rather shy of approaching their schools to hear a teacher's viewpoint. Other teachers, both primary and secondary, kindly filled in questionnaires, from which I have compiled the following comments, opinions and advice.

PRIMARY SCHOOL TEACHERS

What reactions do children in school have to a change of circumstance at home?

Reactions at school to separation or divorce are varied. The children are often clingy or insecure. They may suffer a loss of confidence or concentration. They may become quiet and withdrawn. They sometimes seek extra affection and confidential chats.

How do teachers deal with these reactions?

With patience, care, sympathy and understanding. Teachers aimed to give the children the extra attention they demanded, but tried to be natural with them. They discuss things with the children freely if they wish, and give them extra responsibility, such as special tasks and little jobs, to help rebuild their confidence.

Are their reactions comparable to those following the death of a grandparent?

Some teachers said it was very similar, one said it was much worse, others felt that it depends upon the circumstances of the separation and how much contact the child continued to have with both his/her parents.

Is there any difference in reaction if a sibling is at the school?

The majority felt that it helped, that they could support each other, that it gave them added security and somebody to discuss things with. One teacher felt that it highlighted the situation as otherwise school could be a total escape.

Is there any difference in reaction if their teacher is male/female?

Teachers unanimously felt that they are individuals with individual responses regardless of their sex. Some teachers are more sympathetic than others. Some relate more closely to the children than others. 'We are all different in our approaches.'

Is there any difference in the effects on boys/girls?

Commonly teachers felt that boys show their feelings less, perhaps even try to hide them. Girls were reported to be more emotional, wishing to talk more and enjoying extra affection at this time.

Does it affect the teacher/parent relationship?

Parents are as individual as teachers and the way that they relate is an individual matter rather than a circumstantial one. Some divorced parents do approach teachers for help and advice, just as some conventional parents do. The only time the situation may be difficult is if there is a problem about access which intrudes onto the school premises.

What help is available in schools if problems arise?

Primary teachers stressed the benefits of their informal contact with parents and indicated that the 'open door' policy – easy contact on an informal or formal basis – was the first course of action. Sometimes a social worker may become involved if the family is in difficulty. If a child's behaviour was severely disrupted he would probably be referred for child guidance treatment.

Do you note any differences in children of long-term single parenthood and conventional families?

There was a mixed reaction to this question. The initial reaction tended to be that there was no noticeable difference. But, on reflection, they usually decided that there could be long-term behaviour difficulties if the separation was particularly stressful, or if the lone parent found difficulty in coping with the situation.

How can newly separated parents help their children at school?

Teachers felt parents should inform the school at an early stage so that the teachers are aware of the situation. Parents should talk to teachers and to the children openly to avoid the burden of secrecy, and discuss with the child any problems they might be experiencing with schoolwork or peers because of the situation. The teachers also advised parents to attempt to keep to the same routine as before; keep as many things constant as possible; avoid confrontation in front of the children and try not to play the children off against the other parent.

SECONDARY SCHOOL TEACHERS

How do you usually first learn of separation/divorce?

Secondary school teachers learnt of separation/divorce from a variety of sources and in a variety of ways, such as the education welfare officer, sometimes the child would move away from home temporarily, from the child himself, from pupil records, when taking details for registration or when discussing other problems with pupils.

How do the children react at school?

It proved difficult to generalise in answer to this question because reactions are so varied. Some children get very upset, some become preoccuppied, others may have behaviour problems. Sometimes children bring their unhappiness into school, others see it as a place to get away from the troubles. Occasionally pupils run away if they are very unhappy. Some children were reported to try and play off mother, father and school! For some the change in their circumstances brings them relief from strife, and they react well, increasing in confidence.

How do teachers deal with these reactions?

They may write to the parents, invite the parents to the school to talk, or talk and listen to the child. They may have to resort to support services, the educational welfare officer, social workers or the child guidance service.

Is there any difference in reaction if there is a sibling at the school?

It may depend on the age of the sibling. They sometimes support each other. There is sometimes tension if one child is with one parent and another with the other parent – especially if there is a difference in living standards.

Do you notice any difference in reaction in girls/boys?

Girls tend to show their feelings more and are likely to confide in a close friend whereas boys are not likely to. Age-wise, ten to fourteen year olds produce the most reaction. It is stressful for the over-fourteens, but they are more likely to understand a bit better.

Is there ever any bullying or cruelty because of a child's circumstances?

Answers to this question varied. The majority of adults and children that I spoke to thought not. Here are some of the other answers:

> 'Occasionally there can be bullying or even cruelty, as there also is in two-parent families. If the child reacts tearfully, other children may play on the weakness.'

'One-parent families are fairly commonplace and seem
to be accepted and understood, so bullying is rarely the
case. Occasionally it may arise if a child is in a children's
home.'

Is there any difference at parents' evenings?

No difference was noticed at all. It is the custom for only
one parent to attend for a variety of reasons. There is
definitely no need for self-consciousness.

*Do you note any differences in children of long-term single
parenthood and conventional families?*

Secondary teachers seemed to be tuned in to the financial
difficulties that one parent families might face – presum-
ably because school uniform and equipment are so expensive at this age that shortages are more apparent than in
primary schools. Sometimes a difference is noticed in
attitude to discipline and authority:

'As the child gets more independent he may react
against the system by becoming difficult to handle,
especially if mother is finding it hard to cope with the
day to day problems of life.'

What advice would you give to parents in this position?

Let the school know what the position is so that if there
are any reactions from the child the behaviour can be
immediately recognised and understood. If the split is
acrimonious let the school know who has custody so that
the child is safe and protected. Do not use the children as a
weapon or go-between. Do not try to use the children to
score points off each other or allow the children to do the
same with parents. Try not to influence your child's
feelings about the other parent negatively. Do not stop
disciplining children – especially mothers with sons!
Other suggestions that secondary teachers offered were as
follows:

'Help to make children feel less guilty and embarrassed by talking to the school. Children often feel that they must not be disloyal to parents by talking about home circumstances.'

'Do not allow other distractions, such as work or relationships, to displace finding time to talk to and listen to your children when they want to communicate with you. This may be at the most unwelcome time.'

'Do the same as families with both parents – be supportive, interested, involved, and listen.'

A WORD FROM AN INFANT SCHOOL TEACHER

How do you usually first hear of divorce/separation?

Quite often from the children themselves. Quite often they'll come and tell us that something's happened – that they've got a new Daddy, or Daddy's moved away – very often from the children. Sometimes we hear from people with local contacts who work at the school. But mostly from the children, and then within a few days you find that the parents themselves will come and tell us. They usually come up fairly quickly.

Do you prefer to be told first, or should parents approach the head teacher?

It doesn't matter, as long as we get the news on a fairly reliable basis, and not on hearsay. It is helpful to know the dates when something is likely to happen.

What reactions do children in school have to a change in circumstance at home?

Quite often they are withdrawn and quiet, especially the girls. Initially they are usually quite happy and cheerful about it, if something has been explained to them – that something is going to happen – I'm going to stay with Granny for a bit, or Daddy's moved out for a bit, or whatever it is. Normally they will say it in a very reasonable way, because it has been explained to them. Possibly some weeks later the implications sink in, and then the girls tend to go very quiet. Later they get accustomed to it. They get used to the idea. At first they may come up for lots of extra cuddles. School remains the same, remains stable while there are changes at home. School is an oasis of normality.

Are their reactions markedly different from those following the death of a grandparent?

Yes, because its a longer term thing. They often do come up and say that a grandparent has died. I've had little children coming in and crying about that. I've never had anyone come and cry about what's happened at home. The grandparent thing tends to pass a lot more quickly, the other is a much deeper thing and has a longer effect.

How does it affect your relationship with parents?

You naturally try to be sympathetic. I think they turn to us for advice and guidance. I can think of two or three who have come up and said that they have got problems. Mothers worry about whether they are fulfilling both roles adequately and wonder if their sons are behaving all right in school. Their behaviour has always been all right. There was one little boy whose mother was worried, and I think had some problems herself. We encouraged her to rely on her parents who were very supportive.

What advice would you offer newly separated parents to minimise the effect on their children?

Not to unburden their problems on to the children any more than they can help. Keep the explanations as factual as possible. Try not to be emotional about it. It does worry them who is going to collect them from school and where they will be staying that night, so do be very clear about that, otherwise they feel very insecure. Try not to change the arrangements. If it's the same person every day they are much happier. It's surprising how little children, under seven, worry about what is going on at home. Very often it will upset them if mother goes out to work, even though she is back in time to collect them from school. The fact that they are not actually at home while the child is at school has a very unsettling effect on the child. You wouldn't think it would matter. They like to visualise things going on at home as they know it. Always leave up to date contact numbers so that you can be reached in emergencies.

Is there ever bullying or cruelty because of a child's situation?

I have got very young ones and they are usually very kind to one another at this age – very supportive.

Do you note any differences in children of long-term one-parent families and conventional families?

Odd ones, yes. They vary so much. Some single parents get such a lot of help and support from family that it goes towards making up for it. I can think of others who have a pretty limited experience outside school – not enjoying normal family outings – probably because they cannot afford it. We sometimes notice that boys brought up by their mothers only have been quite unruly, not so much in school, but we hear what happens out of school. I have not found that their schoolwork suffers. I do not think I would ever be able to tell from schoolwork.

Is there any difference at school functions?

It depends on the parents whether they are interested enough to come or not. My experience is that they make an extra effort.

4   Sharing the Care

The question of who should care for the children initially
was not in dispute in most of the cases I researched. Most
custodial parents felt that it was only natural and auto-
matic that their children should be with them. Mothers
automatically expected to have the children. Fathers left to
care for the children wanted custody, but there tended to
be an element of bitterness tinged with judgement about
their ex-wives' perceived inadequacy as mothers:

'I had made that decision a long time ago. In our
relationship I felt that I was the more stable and secure
parent of the two. I'm not saying I was a better parent,
or that she was a bad parent, but it was better for John
to be with me.'

'She would rather leave it to me. She would have been
no good with him anyway.'

'There was no decision to make. She had left the
children. I was going to have them.'

Thus begins the long and often harrowing wrangle
between parents. It can be easy to judge matters as black
and white. The ultimate truth is more likely to be lurking
behind a misty grey. When considering the care of the
children their interests should always come first. Whatever
one parent has done or said to another, their children
should not be denied free and unembittered association
with both parents, so long as they are both willing and
eager to give it.

CUSTODY AND THE COURTS

Although the actual care of the children was more or less automatically decided, when the matter was brought before the court is was sometimes seen as a battle to be won or lost by one or both parents. Most commonly a father would be awkward and obstructive to the court procedure, although there would be nothing to be gained by it:

'The solicitor asked if he had any objections to full custody to me. He took too long to return the forms. Someone from the court had to collect them.'

'He was opposed to me having custody, but he was just using it as a battlefield. In the event he never offered any objections to my sole custody.'

In two cases where mothers had walked out on their families and not contacted them for twelve months and eighteen months respectively they then put up a fight for custody of their children. It can be difficult to understand the motives behind such requests – is there a genuine concern for the child's welfare, or is it a need in the parent to have his/her children restored, and if so, is it justifiable to meet that need?

When there is disagreement between parents about who should have custody the judge will normally ask for reports to be made to help him make a decision. These reports will be made by social workers, or in some cases by the conciliation services. Each parent is interviewed and the children's wishes are sought. Wherever possible this is done in an informal setting. It may be that the school is contacted, or interviews arranged at the school on neutral ground. These days all interested parties, such as grandparents if they have a lot to do with the children, can be involved in the discussions.

It can be a harrowing experience trying to justify your wishes for the care of your child to relative strangers, especially when you may be suffering emotionally in other ways too. In the event, however, the recommendations in the reports do not always materialise. This happened in two of the cases I researched. In the first case there was a daughter aged twelve. Both parents applied for custody and a welfare officer interviewed them all, individually and together. The mother had cared for the child throughout the process of separation, which had taken about two years, and could see no reason for the father to suddenly have her. For his part, he was not really in a position to care for her himself, but was proposing that she would spend much of her time with his own parents. In an effort to be fair to her partner and to remain as objective as possible the mother took pains not to try to influence what her daughter said:

> 'I strode to make her unbiased and emphasised that she need not say things against him. I did not want her to feel used by me at a later date.'

Nevertheless, this mother was amazed when the welfare officer recommended joint custody, and did wonder if she had erred on the side of generosity. It is almost impossible for an outsider to judge accurately how 'worthy' a parent is. Given the comparatively short time that they have to assess a situation, however skilled a social worker is there must be a lot of unknown elements, and their decisions are only opinions in the end. If a decision goes against you at this or a later stage, try not to be too embittered. Instead aim to prove that you can and will care for the child by welcoming those opportunities you are given and making the most of them. Things can often change rapidly at this stage and you may find that you are needed sooner than you think. In the above case the father dropped his application for custody. The mother was given sole custody and the father allowed free access. Although angered by the social worker's recommendations, the mother did not let this come between her and her ex-partner:

66

'I emphasised that he could visit whenever it suited them both.'

Similarly in the case of a father left to care for his two daughters aged six and ten. When the mother applied for custody after barely any contact for nearly two years the conciliation services invested a lot of time and effort into working out what would be best for the children. After interviews with all parties, separately and together, and seeing the children at school, they recommended that the father had custody, but that the children should spend plenty of time with their mother, including part of every school holiday. In the event, just before the court hearing, the elder daughter decided that she wanted to live with her mother. The father could see no wisdom in trying to keep her against her will, so he dropped his application for custody and the child went to live with her mother. The younger child, now age fourteen, rarely sees her mother or her sister as holiday arrangements for exchange visits have never worked out in practice. Try to be open-minded about disappointments such as these. Life and children can be very unpredictable.

An unwelcome element in custody arrangements can sometimes be the financial one. As we see in other sections of the book, both children and money are sometimes used as weapons between parents, and the two combine in a particularly nasty way when a parent applies for custody of a child merely for the financial gain of the maintenance and other allowances. Harry was left to care for his three children, boys aged fourteen and ten, and a daughter aged six. When the case came to court the mother applied for and gained custody of the daughter, in view of her age and sex. Once again, what happens in practice is not exactly what was intended by the recommendation of the court. Although the daughter sleeps at her mother's house each night from Monday to Friday, the father in fact looks after her in every other way. He has her each day after school until bedtime, every weekend Friday to Sunday, all school holidays, and at times of sickness. He takes the child to the doctor and dentist when necessary. He cares for the child willingly and lovingly, and the arrangements suit the mother, who, because of the court ruling, receives family allowance for the child. In theory she could also claim maintenance for herself but she does not as the father is unemployed, to enable him to care for all three children. However, she may claim other allowances from the state. The bitterness that this creates between the parents is enormous, and must cause tremendous insecurities in the young child who relies on both for her stability.

Sometimes financial affairs fall very unfairly. If you can get by on what you have and if your child is happy and healthy, think carefully about your motives before investing time, energy and emotion into trying to get more money out of your ex-partner.

ACCESS

As in so many other areas, access – how it works and how successful it is – is a very individual thing. In none of the cases was there a routine pattern of visiting on certain days of the week. In four cases where the children are now teenagers there are very flexible arrangements whereby they see the second parent at times convenient to both. This varies quite a lot in itself. One of the fathers travels away a lot and so is not often available anyway. Another lives a long distance away so has to be visited on a 'holidays only' basis. In the other two cases the second parents live relatively nearby and see quite a lot of their children. In only one of these cases were behaviour problems noticed as a result of access:

'She lives a bus ride away and has any reasonable access. She sees him once every week or two. He's not bothered. When he returns he gives me back-chat. Our mum [grandparent] has the same. I think it's because

she's aggressive. If he says something she'll get in a
fighting mood. He jumps back. She's got a foul mouth
as well.'

Consistency in your care and standards is paramount at
such times. You cannot change your ex-partner and it is
not usually in the child's interests to stop access. Do not
be drawn into criticising your ex-partner, simply re-state
your own standards and expectations. Providing that you
are firm and consistent the message will eventually get
through and the child will recognise each of you for what
you are.

I know of one case where the only daughter of a couple
would spend every weekend with her father, who was not
regarded very highly by her mother. She would return
each Sunday night with glowing reports of his wealth,
generosity and indulgence. This was a source of regular
aggravation to the mother who was struggling to manage
financially and carrying the main burden of child-care
without enjoying any of the 'perks' that her ex could
offer. In many ways she resented losing the company of
her daughter at weekends and saw it only as a concession
to her ex-partner's selfishness. As the years went by the
child grew more objective and started to judge her father
more critically. At this the mother was suddenly panic-
stricken lest the child should lose all allegiance to her
father who, she then realised, was really a considerable
asset in sharing the care. She unexpectedly found herself
coming to his defence in an attempt to maintain his esteem
in the child's eyes. It can be difficult to remain fair and
objective throughout these times, but it is vital for the
long-term stability of the children.

In some cases there is a lot of contact in the early days
and then for some reason it drops off. Quite often the
second partner tries to use access visits to get to see their
ex:

'My ex-husband wanted to have access to me as well as
the children and stopped coming when it was made clear
that I didn't want to see him.'

In this case elaborate arrangements were in fact made
whereby the children were left at a friend's house from
where their father could collect and deliver them. It can be
an enormous strain for you to see your partner when you
are feeling emotionally low and not entirely in control of
yourself in their presence. Try not to transfer this strain to
the children in trying to protect yourself. Use a friend to
help you when your partner comes, but do try to be there
too. In front of witnesses you will both tend to be on your
best behaviour and although artificial in a way, it is better
than the disgruntled or graceless behaviour that one or
both of you might otherwise display. It may be a big favour
to ask of a friend or relative to attend regularly at these
times, but it is a very important one. Eventually, when a
pattern evolves and good manners are an established habit
the need for a chaperone will disappear.

Other causes of breakdown of access were cited as bad
behaviour from the parent and trying to gain information
from the children:

'He doesn't see them now. They don't want to see
him because of certain incidents. If they should go all he
does is ask questions about me'

Obviously children do let drop tit-bits of information
when in the company of the 'other' parent and it would
be wrong to burden them with keeping things secret. Try
to talk to your ex about this in a reasonable way, on the
phone, when the children are not there. Explain that you
do not want your ex to worry the children by asking them
to guard their words, but that s/he should not take
advantage of the child to gain information. In any case,
you should be prepared to phone and tell your partner
anything material. If the children realise that you keep in

touch and keep them reasonably informed of any developments, it makes them more relaxed and secure. In some cases your partner may be so unreasonable that this is out of the question. Rather than jeopardise the access visits seek help from the conciliation services, or if your children are very young the social services, to see if visits can be supervised in some way – perhaps at a family service unit, or your partner persuaded to become more reasonable.

In one case where relations between the estranged partners had been bitter and strained for two to three years the atmosphere betweeen them suddenly evaporated for no apparent reason. The custodial mother had persisted in keeping her behaviour regular and consistent from the start. Her husband's behaviour had often been unreasonable and erratic. For a long time it was very difficult to make arrangements for visits or to discuss anything about the child:

> 'He put up a barrier to communication with me. We couldn't discuss anything about our daughter. We made arrangements through her. We didn't talk to each other.'

Sometimes this sort of pattern becomes so well established that the children themselves get quite acclimatised to it and can even create barriers to correcting the situation:

> 'She got used to this and became very uncomfortable at the thought of me communicating directly with him.'

You must use your own judgement concerning the right moment to approach your partner about things and do not be influenced by what your child says. Their immature emotions and desire to protect you both can sometimes lead them to misguidedly keep you at loggerheads:

> 'He decided to communicate for no apparent reason. I carried on regardless, unchanging. I think it must have

71

been easier in the end to be pleasant than to continue
hostilities.'

Be careful to remain on an even keel if you do enjoy a
re-opening of communications. If you have been relying
on your child to carry messages back and forth they may
be confused and hurt if this suddenly ceases. If they are
very young they may fear that you will no longer love them
now that they are not needed as a go-between, and they
may even try to obstruct good relations with your ex-
partner. Try to understand how your child feels in this
situation and to remain even tempered and good-
humoured. Reassure them of your own and your partner's affection for them and keep them the main topic of
your exchanges, at least in the early days. It will only
aggravate matters if you suddenly become very pally,
exchanging news, views and general chit chat. Eventually
you may find that you are able to do just that, but let it
happen gradually so that the child can feel certain that
s/he remains your first concern.

Over-indulgence by the second parent often gives rise to
concern, especially when money is normally in short-
supply. It can be infuriating when, after weeks of con-
ditioning the child not to keep asking for things and
explaining that this, that or the other cannot be afforded,
s/he turns up on the doorstep with an even bigger or better
version of the offending article after a trip out with dad.
This is basically another ground rule to be sorted out
between the parents. You cannot blame the child for
having a go. What child wouldn't? Of course you can tell
the child not to ask for things, but that really is not a
problem if both parents have agreed on what is reasonable
and what is not. Grandparents may have to be involved in
this pact too. There is a real danger that bitterness will
creep into relationships if one party feels that the other is
trying to buy the child's affections. It will achieve nothing
in the long run and can lead to an unnecessary breakdown
of access:

'He saw them for about six months. It was upsetting
our daughter. He would take them to his parents and
they seemed to try and buy her favours. I did not want
him to have access because of the upset, and the divorce
court went along with me.'

Breakdown of Access

Access can break down for a number of reasons. The
age-old one of reliability is still common:

'On lots of occasions he said he would pick them up
and then did not turn up. They have waited all day at
the window for him, and when told about it all he said
was "ah".'

Since, generally speaking, some contact is better than
none, you should do your best to minimise the disappointment if your ex is regularly unreliable. It is probably wisest
not to warn your child of the expected visit. Although this
is undesirable in some ways and inconvenient, it is preferable to letting the child down at the last minute. If it means
that they have to go out in old clothes or cut short
something that they have just started this is far preferable
to the hurt of the disappointment.

Also, protect yourself from the same disappointment.
You will be wanting your partner to arrive not only for
their sake, but for the welcome break it gives you. If you
know your partner to be unreliable do not make plans to
do something when you expect him. If you are let down it
will make it harder not to show your feelings and upset the
children. It may seem most unfair that you cannot depend
on these occasional breaks, but knowing that to be the case,
ensure that you arrange a break in some other form soon
after each expected visit. Save hard to pay for a babysitter
and book up to go somewhere different – local entertainment is cheapest and often quite a good standard. Or go
round to a friend for a uninterrupted heart to heart. It
may seem extravagant to pay for a sitter for such a simple

task, but it is an important change of scene and relaxation of responsibility for you.

However, these are only first-aid measures to minimise the effect of the ongoing problem. To cure the situation you need to put the record straight with your partner. Sadly some people just cannot appreciate the importance of reliability in these circumstances and you may well need help from a third party, perhaps a social worker or conciliation officer, to get the point across.

Sometimes things seem to go quite well for a time and then for some reason arrangements break down. In one case the actual separation seemed to have relieved a lot of the tension and aggression between the parents and visits were going quite well. After a time though, the underlying struggle for dominance started to show through and the original problems in the marriage were re-created:

> 'Every fortnight they would go up to the flat and sometimes stop for the weekend. At first they got on better with him. Things were OK for the first couple of years. We even all went swimming together. But then things just drifted back. He was telling me what to do. He was just trying to take over again.'

It is important to remain constant in your relations with your ex-partner. Unless a reconciliation is what you are seeking you must keep the objects of any visits or outings in perspective. Pleasant and enjoyable as it can be to share time together again this can lead to unpleasant side-effects if one partner is still harbouring hopes of a reconciliation and the other is not. It can be cruel and misleading. Far better to maintain a good friendship at a distance, but to discuss the children often and freely on the phone, or over a coffee, in uncompromising circumstances. Be fairly business-like, and if you are going out or expecting a visitor, say so, but arrange another time to chat. Persistence and constancy are important. It can be a very difficult line to tread, and inevitably if one or other of you suffers upsets in your personal life this may reflect in how you relate to each other. Ideally though, it should not. Your contact is for the benefit of the children and if you can maintain it on a level it can be very satisfactory in the long term, and of great worth to the health and happiness of the children.

In the case cited earlier, where a mother left her partner shortly after the birth of their child because of his aggressive dominance, and the fact that he became a Muslim, they too enjoyed a renewal of their relationship whilst they were living separately. For two to three years they saw each other more or less every weekend. However, when the father married into his religion, the mother felt that the influence would be too strong upon the young child and access was stopped:

'It was left up to me to say when and how she would see her father. She sees him rarely now. She hasn't seen him for two years because he moved out of the country. She'll talk very positively about Daddy, although he doesn't keep in touch at all.'

Sometimes the reverse happens and there is no contact at all for a considerable time and suddenly, out of the blue, something alters that. In the case of the young boy whose mother left and made no contact at all with him for twelve months, he was brought face to face with her for the first time at an informal meeting at court. His father describes the reunion:

'For the first half-hour he would have nothing at all to do with her, but as time went on and he realised that I was talking to her, he felt more comfortable. After that we came out and I suggested that we all go to the park. Then I suggested that I go and have a coffee while he carried on around the park with his mum. When they came back he was over the moon. It took no time at all for the link to be re-formed. They came back with their arms around each other, and he asked if he could go and stay with her at the weekend.'

75

He did indeed spend the weekend with his mother, and at time of writing has seen her on two further weekends. On the last visit he phoned up and asked to be collected early because he was 'bored out of his head'!

It is not uncommon for children to be bored, and just as common when they are visiting second parents as at other times. There can be a tendency for separated parents to feel anxious and guilty if their children express these sentiments. Use your discretion as to whether the plea for entertainment is warranted or not. Obviously children do need to be occupied a lot of the time, and younger children more so, but do not allow yourself to be bullied into providing a frenzied round of one treat after another. Often the child bored at your house will return to your partner's house and be equally bored. Again, unite with your partner in an agreement not to be emotionally blackmailed into treats. You may have to make an extra effort to invite school-friends, cousins or company of some other form. You will of course want to take your child swimming, to picnics or puppet shows at certain times, but do not fall into the habit of excessive treats which will be hard to reverse after a time.

JOINT CUSTODY

Most commonly, when parents agree to joint custody, one parent is awarded daily care and control of the child, and quite often cares for the child all week. The other parent sees and cares for them as often as possible, frequently every weekend, sometimes in the week too. Increasingly though, parents living close to each other really do share the care of their children. Obviously the nearer the parents live to each other the better this works. Where the separation has been reasonably amicable and parents still maintain a fairly good relationship this arrangement can work to everybody's advantage. It may take a little while for the children to adapt to having two homes, but once they do they can reap benefits from this rather than feeling disadvantaged. It is more important than ever for each parent to be consistent in their ways and one drawback is that if there is an upset in the relationship or arrangements it is not so easy for the child to get away from the situation. The arrangement is far more common than it used to be, and will probably become even more so as the divorce rate gallops on. It probably works most smoothly where both parties are financially independent and well provided for so that standards of living are more or less comparable and there is no jealousy or bitterness between the parents.

MAINTENANCE

Once the matter of who should have custody is settled, there are rules laid down about how much maintenance should be paid by the non-custodial parent, according to the age of the child, and more particularly the respective incomes of the parents. Your solicitor will advise you of the amounts in your case. Where there is joint custody, 'care and control' of the child is awarded to the parent who is judged to have the child majority of the time and they are entitled to draw the family allowance and single-parent benefit if applicable. If there is disagreement about which parent should have this entitlement, disputes can be settled by applying to the Department of Social Security in Newcastle-on-Tyne and if necessary to the Social Security Commissioners for a decision.

Several people found that no sooner had they settled the battle of who should have custody, than they faced another hurdle in trying to gain some maintenance from their ex-partners for the children:

'I asked for financial assistance from her somehow. She said she couldn't afford it.'

77

'A maintenance order was made for me and the
children. He never paid it.'

Delaying tactics and obstructive behaviour seems to be
prevalent at this time:

'He wouldn't send the books to be examined to
determine maintenance, and when he did they were
obviously false.'

'I was told by the woman who was living with my ex-
husband that he was lying to the court over finances. He
was going back and laughing at getting away with this.'

Unfortunately some people are willing to perjure themselves in order to escape realistic maintenance payments.
This can be very difficult to prove and it can be frustrating
and distressing when you suffer hardship as a result. Your
best ally is a good solicitor (*see also* page 161 for suggestions
on finding one). Amongst those I spoke to, once the battle
was over and amounts agreed, payments usually followed
regularly:

'He did not co-operate for a few weeks but then it was
made a standing order.'

'After we'd agreed he didn't pay until there was a
court order. Since then I get it weekly.'

If either parent's circumstances change an application
can be made to vary the order, in other words to alter the
amount of maintenance. Make sure that you get good
advice on your financial entitlements – use the One Parent
Helpline – the advice is free and it can make quite a
difference to your circumstances to receive your proper
entitlements. After several years struggling on low maintenance payments Gina finally found a solicitor who
managed to negotiate a substantial increase for the
children:

'With a large maintenance increase negotiated about four years ago things have improved a bit for us. Our standard of living has improved considerably.'

STATE BENEFITS

If someone liable to pay maintenance is unemployed, then their partner, assuming that they have no other income, will receive state benefits. Applying for benefits and sorting out entitlements is rarely straightforward or trouble-free, but generally speaking after the initial period, payments are paid regularly with no problems. How well families survive on what they are allowed depends to some extent on their previous standard of living. Apart from the single parent allowance which is paid in addition to family allowance, other benefits are the same as other families in a position of need. Where families were already living on state benefits prior to the separation they did not face any new financial hardship:

'He was unemployed so it did not really affect me'

'I haven't had any financial problems because he's unemployed. I haven't got that worry.'

Quite often there are other concessions for single parents such as council schemes for home insulation, or council leisure and recreation facilities. People seemed to find that they could manage on their state benefits, although they would be in difficulty if faced with a financial emergency. In that case they usually replied that they would turn to their own parents, in one case 'panic', and in another 'cry'!

One person's financial problem can be another person's luxury. The people I spoke to came from a wide cross-section of the community and their standards of living varied considerably. In addition, their previous expectations and hopes for themselves and their children in the future had a considerable influence on whether they felt hard done by in their present circumstances:

> 'I realise that many single parents face these problems, but you have to understand that my ex-husband is very wealthy now . . .'

and of course the nature of the relationship, or lack of it as time goes by, influences one's feelings too:

> '. . . he does nothing for the children apart from what he is forced to do by the court, not even sending them a birthday or Christmas card'

When talking about ongoing financial difficulties most people referred to things such as clothes and shoes:

> 'my son was thirteen before he had a new pair of underpants, having had cast-offs from his cousins until then.'

> 'shoes came down from the fitted ones to the cheapest ones.'

> 'I once had a 'single payment' for shoes and one for school uniforms. It affected me psychologically. I felt I was begging.'

New rules mean that you can no longer apply to the Department of Social Security for a single payment to cover the cost of an expensive 'one-off' item. Instead applications can be made for money from the social fund, which in some cases has to be repaid as an interest free loan. Details of this can be obtained from your local Department of Social Security office, or use the Free-line Social Security. Also you can phone the National Council for One-Parent Families, who will send you an explanatory leaflet.

As the children get older problems tend to become

greater, although this also applies to traditional two-parent families as well:

> 'While it is possible to buy clothing at markets and in sales for young children, teenagers want fashionable "named" clothes. They want to keep up with their friends. They are in adult sizes and to buy "good" shoes has been impossible.'

I did not press people to disclose their financial circumstances and can only comment in a general sense. People seemed to suffer fluctuations in their financial lives. Often there was an initial period of hardship, followed by some stability, followed by a long-term shortfall in financial goals. Much depended on the lone-parent's ability to achieve gainful employment as the children grew older.

Make sure that you are claiming all your entitlements either from the state or from your ex-partner. It can make a big difference. Seek help from a solicitor, the Citizens Advice Bureau, One-Parent Family Advice Line, or the Department of Social Security.

A WORD FROM THE 'OTHER' PARENT

I have included two interviews with 'second' parents, to give a glimpse of shared care from the other viewpoint, and for people to judge for themselves the most helpful attitudes and actions to make sharing the care work. In both these cases the fathers have a lot to do with their children, although the mothers bear the main burden of child-care. I have not attempted to analyse the replies, except to point out that the parents' attitudes to each other can have a considerable affect on how the children relate to each of the parents, and this is borne out in the 'child' case studies later.

The second interview is particularly interesting from the point of view of standards of behaviour, and conflict or confusion of values. Some of the long-standing lone parents whose children rarely or never see their fathers feel that one of the big compensations for bearing sole responsibility for their children is that there is never any dispute over discipline, standards or values. As there is only one of them, things remain consistent and unvarying, and this, they feel, gives a strong element of security to their children. The second father in this section suggests another side to that argument, and I tend to agree with him that children can accept different rules from different parents, just as they know that there may be different rules at school or at their grandparents. So long as their parents are living separately the children can probably cope with the differences, *but* it is essential the children know that each parent will support the other in decisions made when the children are in their care. Obviously problems might arise when parents living together disagree on such matters, or when a single parent starts a new relationship with a partner who may see things differently from him/her, as expressed by this single mother:

'There are difficulties with my current partner which is making me see clearly the importance of remaining a single parent, rather than going into a family situation. I fear the influence of values I don't agree with on Anna, and the loss of control and potential for conflict or confusion in this situation.'

Case One

In this case the parents separated after twelve years of marriage. Divorce proceedings are still in progress although they have lived apart for two years. The children involved are a boy, now aged eight, and a girl, now aged four. The intention is that the parents should have joint custody, with care and control vested in the mother.

How often do you see the children?

I see the children at least twice every week, on average.

82

Sometimes more, sometimes less. I take them on holiday and for weekends.

How long did it take for a pattern to evolve or settle?

It evolved immediately. I was determined that I should not be deprived of access to the children, so even in the first four or five days after separation I went back to see the children to take them out, even though it was exceedingly difficult.

How would you describe those first few times when you took the children out?

Well, I don't remember much about the act of taking the children out. There weren't any awkward questions from the children. We had talked to them about it before and they understood as far as they could. I think in some ways it was a relief that the tensions were being dealt with, that something was happening differently. The difficulties were that my ex-wife refused to accept the situation, and to a degree I don't think now, two years later, that she's accepted it. She only very, very occasionally phoned me to discuss it, and on two occasions wrote me letters which were mindless wanderings. And so she used the opportunity when I picked up and dropped off the children to have a go at me, to say she couldn't understand what was going on, and would I go back, and why didn't I go back, and so on. The children realised what was going on and would either immediately run off into the house, or would become very aggressive or protective towards one or the other of us. The little girl was more emotional, more difficult. The lad understands fully what's going on and realises that his life, to an extent, hasn't changed, and he isn't really that upset.

Have you noticed any changes in the children since the separation?

I obviously don't want there to have been any changes,

because I like to think that they're happy and well-balanced and good children. I don't have any reason to think that they have regressed. There's no evidence of things such as going backwards at school, or failing to make progress, or bedwetting or anything like that. So, I'd like to think that there haven't been any detrimental effects. I may be wrong, but I would like to think that.

Do your children behave differently with you than they do with your ex-partner?

I don't know. I have no evidence to think that they behave differently. Although because my ex-partner may be with them all the time and also possibly weaker than I am as far as ability to dominate is concerned, they may feel that they get away with more with her.

Do you think you behave differently because of your situation?

Oh, yes. I think one over-compensates, over-indulges, is over-emotional and over-affectionate in the time that one has with them.

Did you find it hard to handle your children at first?

No. No problem at all.

Did you find it hard to occupy them at first?

No. No problem. In the early days I bought certain things and encouraged them to leave other things with me. I concentrated on those I knew they would like, for instance with the little girl, colouring books, and with the boy, cars. For £5 you can buy a lot of colouring books, crayons and little tiny cars, so that was not a major problem.

Were you able to accommodate them straight away?

Yes, in so far as I'm very lucky to have a cottage in the country, where we can go at any time, and it sleeps six people, so that's no problem. The flat that I'm now living in has only one bedroom, so when I have the children to stay I take them to the cottage, which is only an hour's drive away. When the matter of the matrimonial home has been resolved I should be in a better situation to accommodate them with me.

Do you ever resent or take it out on them?

No. Although I do believe that our problems started the day that the first child was conceived. The marriage wasn't brilliant before the children, because of differences in background, religion and expectation, and I was as much to blame for that in making the wrong decision as anybody. However, I think that when my ex-wife found she was pregnant, that gave her a totally absorbing new attitude, and my life became increasingly intolerable as the years went by. But I've never ever taken it out on them.

Is your relationship with your ex-wife stable?

It is stable now. It wasn't stable for six or eight months. But it is now, I think, in the sense that it is just icily polite – not too co-operative, just tolerably polite. I fear that there is going to be a period where it is going to get worse when my ex-wife is forced to sort out the property question, as forced she will have to be. That is going to be a problem time.

Do you ever agree modes of behaviour or discuss the children over the telephone?

Yes, we discuss the children over the telephone. On occasions she has told me that I need to speak to one or other because they are very naughty, or not doing their homework, or getting big-headed. We do discuss the children over the phone and we do discuss them when we meet, but it's in a very business-like manner.

Do you think the children ever try to play one of you off against the other?

Yes, but I don't blame them. It probably works.

Do you ever attend parents' evenings, concerts or sports days?

Yes. I have an agreement with their schools that they inform me of the events, and if business allows, I go. It doesn't cause me any difficulty or embarrassment.

How did you inform the school?

I simply wrote a letter to the head of the pre-prep department informing them. Their response was totally disinterested. It happens all the time apparently. I don't mean that they didn't take it seriously, but they didn't show any worries or express concern that they should watch the children very carefully. I think their attitude is that the school is bigger than the child. The school the lad is at now has a house system and the children are encouraged to be loyal to the house, and they are. They love it. My son is totally committed to the house and his responsibility there, and he's in every organisation that he can join.

Has your son become more involved in school activities and do you think that it may have something to do with the situation?

Yes, and I'm sure it could be. It has helped him. He is also very lucky in that he has a terrifically good housemaster, who knows the situation and who I phone from time to time to discuss his general demeanour, attitude and air of commitment to the school and to himself.

Have you found a new partner? How do the children relate to her?

Yes. The children relate to her very well. No problems there at all but when the children go back to their mother and say what a wonderful time they had, that causes problems and I get stupid phone calls asking me not to introduce the children to that woman. However, they haven't met very often. The time that I have with the children I tend to want to spend with just them. I don't want to share that time. I don't want to share it with anybody, let alone her. I would never want her to substitute their mother, no one can take the place of a mother.

How does your ex-wife relate to your new partner?

With tremendous contempt and disapproval, which I find very understandable.

Could this be improved in any way?

I wouldn't want it improved. I don't want them to get on well. What's the point? I think it's terribly important that my ex-wife gets herself sorted out emotionally, mentally, financially and physically, and finds somebody else she can be happy with, if that is what she wants to do.

Would it be a relief to you if she were to find someone else?

I supppose there are sub-conscious feelings of guilt and if she found someone else I suppose those feelings may be assuaged. The worry would be that if she met somebody else, that other person might have an undue influence on the children. If I was unhappy about that situation I would move heaven and earth to get custody.

Do the children still see their grandparents?

Their only grandparents are on my side. They see them as much as before, if not a bit more. My parents didn't and still don't see my ex-wife – that was one of the problems. She would never make any social contact with anyone. She just wanted to live a quiet introspective little life.

Case Two

In the second case the parents separated after fourteen years of marriage, and have been separated (now divorced) for six years. There were two children of the marriage, a boy now aged just fifteen, and a girl now aged eleven. The mother has custody of the children, although as we shall see, their father continues to be very involved with them.

How have the arrangements worked out? How often do you see the children?

In the early stages it was difficult. To start with when I left I simply had a room in another teacher's flat, and although she was very good about it I didn't want to impose. She was quite happy for the kids to come, but obviously there was only one bedroom, so they were in with me. I didn't get much opportunity to see the children in the early stages. But then I moved out and shared with yet another teacher, who had quite a large house in the country, and again he was very good with the children. He loved having them. They used to come and stay with me every other weekend. After about two years I moved into a place of my own, and from then on it was a regular arrangement that they stayed every other weekend, usually from the Friday night to the Sunday night. That was subject to variation at either of our requests. It worked very well. We had the odd dispute, but generally it was OK.

In the very early days did you miss seeing them because of the accommodation problems?

I deliberately made sure that I saw them, as much as two or three times a week, possibly for only twenty minutes. I would meet them off the school bus, because I worked nearby, and walk them home. It was a very important link, because I had left once before and been away for three or four months. My son was five at the time and he was very aware of it. I learnt from that, and tried to improve things the second time. There's no way you can make it easy, but I tried to give them constant reassurance. I tried to make them see that just because I was no longer living with them, I hadn't disappeared off the face of the earth, and I could get to them very quickly if they needed me. I used to speak to them on the phone very often. There was never more than four days without them seeing me, and never more than two days without them having contact with me. My working hours helped a lot.

Have you noticed any changes in the children since the separation?

Well, it's odd really. It's almost as if I was still there. Inevitably the kids occasionally try to play one off against the other. They might tell their mother that they were allowed to stay up late to watch a programme on television. She would ring up and say she didn't approve of them watching that programme, or staying up that late, and that would lead to a discussion as to whether she could dictate to me about what they could watch, or whether I had the right to decide. We arrived at the decision that since I was in charge of them for the weekend it was just as much my right to decide what they should watch. The contact with them has remained so close that it's difficult for me to distance myself from them and see change objectively. Obviously they've changed, as all children do as they grow older, their personalities have developed. The boy is very like I was at that age, whereas the girl is very different. She's quiet and determined and placid. Nothing upsets her. The lad can be a bit wild and a bit boisterous, but so was I.

Can you expand a little on your discussion with your ex-wife over who should decide on the rules when the children are with you?

Where we couldn't agree, then whoever they were with should decide. Obviously as she has custody it is up to her to decide 90% of the time, but if they were staying with me, then I was not going to alter my standards to suit her. If I felt that a particular programme was suitable, or wasn't

89

too late, then I wasn't going to say that they couldn't watch it just because she didn't approve.

Was she able to accept that? In some cases I suspect it might jeopardise the access arrangements.

Well, she didn't really have much option if she wanted me to continue to have the children.

Do your children behave differently with you than they do with your ex-partner?

Possibly. I think on some occasions they do. My son does give my ex-wife problems. He is sometimes moody, or storms around the house, and on one occasion she phoned me up and asked if I could have a word with him. She meant could I go round. I said put him on the phone, and even on the phone I was able to instil sufficient discipline in him to stop doing whatever it was, to behave. He was only being stupid.

Do you think that you behave differently because of your situation?

Differently from what – that's the thing. Whilst I was unattached, yes, I did behave differently, in lots of ways. I recently remarried, and the fact that I have two children by a previous marriage affects this marriage. So, yes, I do behave differently.

Do you over-compensate or over-indulge the children?

No, not really. No, I've deliberately avoided it. It's the worst thing to do, to try and buy their love.

Did you find it hard to handle the children at first? Did you find it hard to occupy them?

No, not at all. We get on so well. They used to look forward to coming to see me and I used to look forward to having them. Money was a problem in the early stages. I couldn't afford to take them to the pictures. If we went to the park I might buy them an ice cream. They would bring some toys with them from home, and basically they both love drawing, and I had plenty of paper and pens. The chap I was sharing with was happy to involve them in what we were doing, so lots of the time we would be working on the cottage and the kids would be carrying bricks, wheeling wheelbarrows, tidying the greenhouse, that sort of thing.

Have pets featured at all?

Yes. After I left my ex-wife got a cat, which is something that probably never would have happened while I was there, and they are both very fond of it.

Do you ever resent or take it out on the children?

No, I don't think so. I don't think I have anything to resent them for. My ex-wife may have.

Do you think she ever resents or takes it out on them?

Yes, I think she probably does. I think she tries hard not to take it out on them, but occasionally it comes through I think.

Is your relationship with you ex-wife stable?

It's stable in the sense that we can be reasonably civilised to one another in short spells. I find that if I have to be with her for more than about fifteen minutes, things deteriorate very rapidly. After that time she starts going over everything and blame starts to be apportioned even now. She still resents the fact that I walked out, quite a lot. Maybe I still feel guilty about the fact that I did. I therefore just do not feel comfortable in the house. We've made our mistakes. The first year she invited me to Christmas dinner. It was awful. The atmosphere was so false. It was purely for the kids. I had to leave earlier than arranged because it was just so awful.

Do you ever attend parents' evenings, concerts or sports days?

Oh, yes. It makes it easier actually. We just split up and do half each and exchange notes at the end. It saves us having to be together. I know my son's form teacher well. My daughter has just started a new school. I pick her up every morning and drive her in to school. I find out what's happening at school while we chat. I know my son's school well.

Do you feel you have a good relationship with both the children?

Oh, yes. Better than I would have had if I'd stayed. It would have been destroyed if I'd stayed. It was really affecting my relationship with them. I think they are as well-balanced a pair of kids as you would wish to come across. The lad occasionally has his outbursts, but compared to most fifteen-year-olds he's a mouse. And the girl is a delight. You couldn't ask for a nicer kid.

Some people feel that children are scarred for life.

Well, however well you know them you can't really get inside even your own kids, can you? I feel sure that they would not have had such a good relationship with me.

Were the children affected by temporary relationships between your marriages?

Yes, I think they were. I had to be very careful with the lad. He was at an impressionable age. I tried hard to avoid mentioning any friends. I didn't want him to get the impression that this was what life was about – a succession of girls that you saw for two or three weeks. I think they saw through it though. There were a couple of girls whom I thought enough of to bring into their lives. So they know there were at least two others before I met my present wife.

How do the children relate to your new wife?

They get on well. Occasionally it creates problems, for instance, when my ex-wife wants me to have the children unexpectedly.

How does your ex-partner relate to your new wife?

Well, they don't really know each other. They've met briefly. It helps I suppose that I didn't meet her until long after we'd split up.

Has your ex-partner got a new partner?

No. She's had one or two, but there's no prospect of a permanent replacement because she is Catholic. Although we are divorced in the civil courts, I think in her own mind she probably still believes that she is married to me. Unless she is successful in getting an annullment I don't think she would allow herself to enter into another permanent relationship. It's one of the sad things about religion.

Is there anything you would like to add?

Yes. The one thing about being separated is that occasionally, not often, but occasionally, you can get this awful panic that you're not there with your children. You may suddenly feel that something has gone wrong. It tends to happen when they are a long way away. It's the one thing that isn't nice – that you are simply not there with them.

5 Discipline – Parents and Children

The issue of disciplining your own behaviour and your children's behaviour is an interesting one, but a difficult one to research because everybody has a different starting point. The people I spoke to were all at different stages along the road of single parenthood. Their children were various ages and the patterns of discipline before their separations were apparently quite different anyway. I also sense that as a very reserved and somewhat proud nation, we find it very difficult to admit to any problems with child rearing. We tend to bring our children up fairly exclusively, often without help from the extended family or other groups. Consequently we may feel that to admit that our children give us problems can only be a reflection of our own shortcomings as parents. In fact there is so little assistance and training for parenthood that it is hardly surprising we are not all experts at it. Most single-parents I spoke to felt that their children behaved no differently from other children, except that perhaps they 'got away with' a bit more.

ARGUING (CHILDREN)

In those cases where there was more than one child the most difficult behaviour parents had to handle was arguing, tormenting, and answering back. Every parent with two or more children will identify with this problem and it can drive one to distraction when their arguments become habitual.

94

'Mike and Jack fight like cat and dog. On their own
they're as good as gold. We've just moved house and
there's a lot to be done. I got to the stage where I got
Mike to bed and I just sat down and cried. Everything
was going wrong and all they could do was play me up. I
try to give them everything I can, treat them and things
and all they do in return is argue.'

If your children are playing you up to the extent that you
are tearful try to be reassured that not everything is going
wrong. Sibling arguments and mischievousness are
normal healthy behaviour, and it sometimes indicates a
measure of recovery by the children that they feel secure
enough to do this. Decide on a course of action and stick to
it. It will pay dividends each time the situation arises. Be
assertive, persist, do not back down, do not give up or give
in. Be strong, do not feel sorry for them or reward bad
behaviour with leniency. Stick to your demands and face
them with love and security. Think how nice it is that they
are behaving normally.

TEARFULNESS AND TANTRUMS (CHILDREN)

Other behaviour described as difficult to handle was
emotional or aggressive tantrums:

'He gets a bit emotional, aggressively emotional. I find
that awkward to handle. He gets a paddy on him and
has a tantrum. I cannot abide them so I send him to his
room'.

It is easy to imagine that every time your child has an
emotional outburst it is directly attributable to your circumstances, especially in the early days. Sometimes it may
be, and if the timing of it makes it apparently so, then
comfort and discussion are the best solutions, in a warm
but matter-of-fact way. Sometimes children behave like

95

this because they are tired or bored, or because they were rewarded for it on a previous occasion. Be confident and firm in your handling, try not to be visibly affected. It can reinforce feelings of insecurity. Provide a distraction in a matter of fact way – not necessarily a game, perhaps a household task. If they cannot apply themselves to this it may be an idea to suggest that they stay in their room until they wish to co-operate. Sometimes a firm and prolonged cuddle can do the trick, even if they are noisy and kicking at first. Even quite big children can respond to this if you are confident that it will work. Hold them firmly and talk through whatever is worrying them. Still ask them to do something co-operative afterwards, perhaps with you. Do not reward them. Confidence is again the key. The more you behave confidently the more confident you will become, and this will help to conquer insecurity in both of you.

SHOUTING AND THREATENING (PARENTS)

Parents of younger children often admitted to shouting a lot. They felt it was worse at times of stress or when they were emotionally affected by other events. This is obviously a normal reaction to stress, but being in a one-parent situation means that you are under a lot of stress and this may lead to excessive shouting:

> 'I shout. Every day I shout. As soon as I wake up I start shouting. I never used to be a shouting person.
> Sometimes they're not even playing up, but I'm that fed up some days, or I'm trying to get so much done, that I end up taking it out on them.'

Those able to confess to shouting also seemed able to laugh about it. In a way they seemed to have it in perspective. They were aware that it was not too good to be shouting all the time, but also recognised that it was a sort of safety valve that prevented any build up of more aggressive behaviour. The more you shout the easier it is to forget about it afterwards. It probably does reduce its effectiveness in time, but it still serves the purpose of relieving the tension for the parent.

Sometimes it happens that when the shouting seems to have no effect parents search in their minds for threats that will frighten the children into good behaviour:

> 'Their dad was very aggressive. They played me up
> that much one day that I said "if you can't behave
> yourself, I'm going to do what your dad did to you." I
> never would, but I find myself saying that to them. Or I
> say, "if you want to play up you can go and live with
> your dad. I've had enough of you." I don't mean it, I
> just say it in temper.'

Sometimes you will shock yourself with the words that come out of your mouth. Do not be overcome by guilt. Carrying a burden of guilt around is far more damaging than the remarks you make. Discuss what has happened and why with your child. They are usually reassured if you explain that you only said whatever it was because you were tired and cross. Do not get over-emotional. Forget the guilt and do not reward your child inappropriately because you feel bad. Often the child will recover quicker than you although their tolerance of threats and conflict in general depends on their past experiences and on their personalities. Many people said how much more they discussed things with their children and what a good effect this had. Try to outweigh the bad times with those of happiness and laughter. Show your child as much love and affection as you can, especially when they are being good. Reinforce good behaviour with lots of praise and encouragement, and try not to expect too much of them because you are on your own – that is something over which they have no control.

THREATS (CHILDREN)

More than one parent reported that at times their children have threatened either to leave home or run away to the other parent. This usually happens as an extention of playing one parent off against another and is most likely to happen if you and your partner are not on the sort of terms to enable you to discuss groundrules for behaviour, expenditure and so on. Most parents recognise that in the long run, given the circumstances, the children have to survive in whichever household they are allocated, and that it is in everybody's interests to support each other rather than to undermine or try to outdo the other. The parents I spoke to were finally and reluctantly driven to call their children's bluff:

> 'They started to play one against the other – "buy this or I'll go back to mum". I stood it for several weeks but then at the end of the day I packed his bags and said "get in the car, I'm taking you back to your mum." He cried his heart out.'

Children often make these sorts of threats – even those from two parent families, the difference is that normally a child does not have an alternative dwelling to make for. (*See also* Chapter 11 – Child One in 'A Word from the Children'.). However, it can be a weak spot that children play on even when there is nowhere to go. The following is a quote from a widow with two children, this one aged eleven:

> 'A couple of times Matthew packed his bags. He's said "I'm leaving home". I've said, "go on then". He says "you don't love me", I say "don't be silly".

CRITICISM OF EX-PARTNERS (CHILDREN)

Sometimes children will tell you heart-rending tales of how cruel and unfair your ex-partner is when they are with them. They probably believe that what they are reporting is true, but quite often it is a passing mood which fades like a cloud in sunshine the next time they set eyes on their other parent or speak to them on the phone. Obviously keep a sharp eye on the situation if you have any genuine suspicion of your partner, but otherwise remain as even and as objective about their rules and behaviour as you would about any relative whose standards your child has to observe.

SMACKING

Parents said that they disliked smacking, avoided smacking, or resorted to it occasionally but found it ineffective. More than one parent admitted smacking children when they themselves were emotionally upset about a problem or relationship. In one case the eldest child was due to babysit the youngest one to enable the father to go out:

'I've only hit the kids once and it really upset me.
Three minutes before I was due to go out he said he
couldn't babysit. He could have told me before. I felt
very guilty about it. It hurt me more than it hurt them.
Now I try and sit down and talk to them.'

It is not unnatural to lash out occasionally at your children when you are at your wits' end, but it is unlikely to help anybody, and may well leave you feeling guilty afterwards. Do not feel weighed down by guilt but do try other methods of discipline. If you find that you are regularly smacking your children you may need help. Approach your local social services or even the NSPCC – they will be glad that you have sought help – or look in your local telephone directory for a parents' or crisis helpline. Seek out other help or support groups by writing to the National Council for One-Parent Families for details of resources in your area.

OTHER FORMS OF DISCIPLINE

The most commonly mentioned form of discipline was the use of discussion. Obviously the facility for this varies with the age of the child and when you are really tired you just will not be able to summon up the energy to go into lengthy explanations. However, if the practice of discussing things is established from a very young age it does become an intrinsic part of family life and helps things run more smoothly. This is far easier where there is only one child. When the child always has an adult's attention, one to one, there is far less need for them to indulge in attention-seeking behaviour. The more children there are the more difficult it can be to discuss things in a calm and civilised way, especially if the children are close in age. Sometimes it is important to make a ruling without prior discussion, just to bring an end to the furore. Try talking about what happened at a later stage when everyone is peaceful – either at the meal-table or at bedtime. Talking through the events of the day at bedtime is a very healthy habit to form anyway. That way your child is assured of your individual attention at least once a day and knows that s/he will have the chance to put his/her point of view. Also, it can be a useful educational exercise for little ones, seeing how much they can remember, and a form of therapy where you both, or all, unwind at the end of a busy day. It reminds you of and reinforces the good times as well as smoothing over the bad.

Several people referred to sending their children to their room and other sorts of deprivation – unplugging the television or video, or not allowing children out for a week. These methods seemed to be effective when parents were confident that they could enforce them:

'I keep him [12 years] in for a night and he doesn't do it again for a good while.'

'I send John [8 years] to bed at six o'clock. He doesn't like that. Or no television for a week, or stay in for a week.'

Personally I have always found keeping in unwilling youngsters, or depriving them of the television counter-productive. It has caused more boredom and friction and been a bigger punishment for me than for them. Perhaps if I had been better able to persist in enforcing these kinds of punishment I might have found that they were more effective.

Of course very young children who are behaving badly are often transformed by the provision of a distraction, or a constructive activity. Older children also respond well to a change of activity or scene. In good weather a walk out, a picnic in the park or a trip to the swimming baths can do the trick. In winter many parents have rediscovered the value of playing board games or doing jigsaws as a joint venture. When shopping for such items make sure that you set aside enough time to investigate the value of the game before you purchase one. Large boxes and glossy pictures often hide flimsy and inferior goods, whereas sometimes comparatively cheap items in fact provide very good value for money.

RESENTMENT (PARENTS)

None of the men felt that they resented their children for their situation, or ever took it out on their children. Most of the women confessed to feeling resentment towards their children at times and to sometimes taking it out on them:

'I think I do sometimes. I don't mean to.'

'Yes, I have done, but I know it's not her fault. I tend to resent society, people's attitude or lack of understanding generally. Judgemental attitudes make me feel worse.'

'I suppose you take it out on them when you are very tired. I did go through a time when I didn't want them because they were his children. Social services frightened me out of that by the word 'adoption'. It brought it home to me that I did want them, that I didn't want to lose them.'

Obviously these kinds of negative feelings about your children are usually very temporary and pass almost as quickly as they appear. Try to remember that the children did not ask to be put in the situation and that they have no control over it. They have to accept a lot of dictates about their life-style without any consultation. Chatting to others in a similar situation can help a lot – join Gingerbread, or look up a parent help-line in your locality. If you sense that your feelings are becoming unreasonably strong, or that you are taking your frustrations out regularly on the children either physically or verbally, seek help. Go to social services or the NSPCC and ask for support. Better to swallow your pride and do this than risk hurting or losing the children.

OVER-COMPENSATING BECAUSE OF YOUR SITUATION

I suspect that there are an alarming number of spoilt, over-indulged and over-compensated children around. There is little doubt that most of the guilt that parents feel about their situation is towards their children – what they would have wished for them ideally both, materially and socially:

'I suppose I do actually spend more money on them
than I ought, trying to give them the life that I think
they would have had, and should have the right to
expect.'

Over and again people confessed to buying all they can,
taking the children out as often as possible, and over-
compensating generally by being too soft with them. If
parents themselves feel especially low or down-hearted the
tendency is to allow the children to get away with things, or
even to give them treats or rewards in order to make them
happy and in turn make the adults feel better. Most people
know in their own minds that this is not the solution to an
unhappy situation. Although occasionally a new toy or
other treat can bring temporary relief to boredom or
unhappiness, in the end everybody has to accept life in
whatever form it comes and gain comfort and security
from talking to each other and sharing affection and
consideration. This is not always easy, but constantly
trying to buy a child's affection or good behaviour is sure
to end in tears when the money dries up, and is not a good
basis for healthy relationships. Only one custodial parent
answered differently:

'I try not to – if anything I over-compensate by being
hard, not giving in materially. I feel I have a balance,
and Anna knows deep down that she has got a lot of
freedom, love and good things from life. I try not to feel
guilty or be influenced by others views on handling the
situation, except for those people whose advice I value.'

6 Housing and Employment

HOUSING

The issue of housing after separation is rarely straightforward. Not only are there all the attendant problems of finance and who should have what, but also the place where people physically stay can play quite a major part in how quickly they recover and start to think positively about the future.

People sometimes surprised me by their reactions to their circumstances in relation to housing. Dennis, unexpectedly left by his wife after twenty years of marriage, did not cope well in other ways. But as far as housing goes he made a snap decision that paid off:

> 'I put the house up for sale and moved out. I had to get out; it held too many memories and hassle. I got 100% mortgage on another house. When the first house was sold I gave her half. I sold the car and gave her half. I bought new furnishings and completely redecorated. I did everything differently. We chose the old furniture together. I chose everything here on my own, except for the child's things. I asked him what he wanted.'

Of course not everybody is in the position to do this and it is always wise to consider big decisions carefully before rushing into them; but in this case it happened to work out. Dennis believes it was the best thing he could have done, and after an initially bad start emotionally, three years later he is moving on from rebuilding his home to rebuilding his life. Holding on to the matrimonial home can sometimes be a way of trying to retrieve the marriage, and in cases where this is not going to happen, it can hamper the healthy development towards a new life.

Peter was left in similar circumstances after twenty-one years of marriage, and still lives in the former matrimonial home, eight years later. He admits to hating the house and spending as much time as he can away from it. Inevitably it holds many memories for him. He admits, too, that he still has a hankering to restore his marriage, even though he now has a lady-friend:

> 'In a way we're better off without her, yet I still miss her. Even now, I've told Jane (lady-friend) I don't know what I'd do if she appeared on the doorstep and said: "It's all over between me and him." I don't know what I'd say.'

Obviously it is good for the children to have as much continuity in as many areas as possible, but if your recovery is hampered by clinging to old possessions and memories of the past it may be better to make a move if you are in a position to do this. New furnishings and a change of scene might benefit you all, and enable you to realise that you can still create a home as a one-parent family.

Sometimes memories are forced upon the family. When a marriage breaks down but neither party will move out, it can lead to a very difficult position where you have to share accommodation with your partner, whilst not associating with them. The strains of this situation cannot be overestimated. It makes it very difficult to parent the children, and often people only survive this period of enforced proximity on the instruction and encouragement of their solicitor:

> 'We were separated in the same house for twelve months. That cracked me up. The solicitor encouraged me to stand my ground.'

> 'He wouldn't move out for ages. I did not want to move because of the child [12 years] but at one stage I

would have willingly done so to get away from him. He
wore me down with aggravation. I was very tempted to
leave at times.'

Whilst it might be desirable to establish a new home once
you have regained emotional stability, it is probably best to
avoid unnecessary moves in the early days. You may have
to rely on the courts to prevent your partner from
molesting or assaulting you or the children. This is obviously an unhappy situation, and whatever the courts rule,
in the end it is your emotions that are battered. Seek help
and support from close friends and groups such as Gingerbread.
  A useful booklet published by the Department of the
Environment and Central Office of Information is 'One-
Parent Families – Help with Housing'. You should find a
copy at council Housing Advice Centres, or the National
Council for One-Parent Families will send you one. The
law is complicated and every case individual. Amongst
those I spoke to people who were buying their own homes
at the point of separation generally seemed to come to
some agreement quite quickly about who should live there
– although money wrangles tended to drag on for long
periods afterwards. People had a variety of experiences of
council housing. Council policies sometimes change, and
recently councils have probably become more accommo-
dating than they used to be, partly because of the changes
in society, and partly because they are trying to improve
their images as landlords.
  Three of the people I spoke to applied for council
housing for the first time when they became one-parent
families. They were applying in different areas at different times and had different experiences. This highlights
the need to get good advice and to use someone to support
you whenever possible. As in all walks of life, council
employees are sometimes tired and short-tempered. They
may sometimes give incorrect information and you need
someone under less emotional strain than yourself to fight

this battle for you. Contact your local Gingerbread, CAB, or use the helpline of NCOP (National Council for One-Parent Families). Go to the local housing aid centre, but if the information seems incorrect get a second opinion. It is most important that you give them all the relevant information. They cannot give correct advice if they are not in possession of all the facts.

In case number one, where Alice had been made homeless by her husband installing another woman in their house whilst she was in hospital giving birth, she went to live with her parents on leaving hospital. She applied for council housing, but her parents would not sign a form saying that they would make her homeless. Alice had to go on the waiting list in the normal way and after six months she was offered a flat 'in a foul area in a foul condition'. Fortunately accommodation was forthcoming from another source, but what the outcome would have been otherwise is unknown.

In the second case mother and baby moved out of privately rented housing because of desperate circumstances. They went on the council waiting list, but in the meantime went into a council squat. She feels that this speeded things up and she was offered a place quite quickly. She did not accept the first offer however, but described the second as excellent.

In the third case the family was in married quarters of the RAF when the marriage ended. The mother tells her own story:

'The local council would not house me – they advised me to return to where I came from. When I enquired there they told me it would be at least three years before they could house me. This caused a lot of stress and actually caused my children and me to be split up. I could not bear the thought of living with my parents so the children went to live with them and I remained in accommodation belonging to my boyfriend. Eventually the relationship broke up and I went to live with my parents, which drove me to the point of suicide and I

107

knew I had to get out. I spent four years running a business and living over it in condemned property which I did not consider a fit home for the children. During this time I decided to send them to boarding school (one parent family scholarships). Eventually when the lease was bought out by property developers we moved into a council house for fifteen months, and I felt more secure than I think I had ever felt in my life. After that time I had a job and was able to buy a house. After all the insecurity this house is very dear to us all.'

Other bad experiences with councils include being made responsible for the absent partner's arrears of rent. Kate changed the tenancy from joint names to her name only. She was not aware that her husband had built up arrears of rent and was not advised of the fact on her application. She became responsible for the arrears and this resulted in an eviction order being served. She had only four days to find the money and had to turn to her mother who took the money out of her building society account. Similarly in another case:

'In the end he was served with an eviction order. The house was signed over to me. This left me with all his arrears, plus the furniture and other things to pay for.'

However, in a further case the woman was only held responsible for half the arrears. Seek help and advice at times like this. Accept as much support as possible and persist in your applications until you receive satisfaction.

Housing Associations

The main function of housing associations is to rent flats or houses to people in need. They provide both purpose-built flats and houses and improved older property. Most associations have a waiting list but they vary in length. If you are in difficulty over accommodation you may find that a local housing association will regard your application sympathetically. Find out where your local associations are from the Housing Advice Centre, CAB, or library and either apply direct or ask your local council to nominate you for a tenancy.

EMPLOYMENT

The problems of employment for most single parents are the same as those faced by most married mothers. Of course there are the additional pressures of relying on one income, the full time and sometimes unrelieved responsibility for the children and the emotional pressures of not having a partner with whom to share one's problems.

Amongst those I researched the person who had always been a full-time 'stop-at-home' mother, and continued to be so, expressed least discontent with her lot. That side of her life was unaffected by the changes in her marital status, except that she now felt free to invite friends and to visit relatives without the worry of incurring her husband's wrath. Two mothers who had not worked previously took part-time evening jobs to try to subsidise their income and to get out of the house. One relied on a baby-sitter, the other her parents, to care for the children in her absence. Not only was it difficult relying on other people in this way, but they both felt very self-conscious about being divorced. Although they did not publicise the fact both felt that it was soon discovered and that male workers quickly took advantage of the fact:

'It was OK getting a job, but it caused problems with the boss who thought I was easy. It makes you very vulnerable. He kept touching me all the time. It caused me to leave in the end.'

'I had a cleaning job, but the men would take advantage. They would assume that you were there for them.'

Sexism and chauvinism at work can be a problem for all women, and if you are feeling below par anyway you may find it harder than ever to deal with. It is insulting and humiliating to be treated as a sex play-object with no rights or feelings of your own. Try your best to be assertive on the subject from the start. Do all you can by body language and straight unemotive talking to dissuade males from taking liberties. Band together with other women to show up badly-behaved men (*see* Chapter 9, page 155 – Assertiveness Training). Watch your own behaviour too. If your workplace is the only place that you can escape the children and enjoy socialising make sure that you are not unintentionally provocative. Of course you are entitled to fraternise freely, but just as men should observe certain standards in their behaviour, so should women.

The biggest restriction to employment for most people is the lack of suitable childcare arrangements. Various options are described in Chapter 1 and in addition some workplaces have day nurseries or creche facilities attached. People often imagine that once a child reaches school age the parent will be free to restart work. Unfortunately the school day is a short one, the holidays long, and children liable to fall sick without notice! Unless you are a school teacher yourself or have a very understanding boss, you will find it difficult to find a job flexible enough to fit in with these criteria. This is a problem for most traditional families too. Perhaps in the future employers might be more realistic about employing parents and allow for more flexibility for both mothers and fathers to make the most of the skills that people have to offer.

An ideal solution one person I researched had hit upon was working in a residential setting where she could do her job quite easily with her child in tow. This solved the problems of housing, employment and childcare all in one go and at the time of writing she has successfully been engaged in this employment for ten years. The disadvantages are that your home is also your workplace. Not only are your duties as a parent unrelenting, but also, unless you are very careful, so are those of the job. Other people who fared best in the circumstances tended to be those who had already established themselves in a strong employment position prior to their separation.

Not surprisingly men tended to fall into this category more readily than the women. One man was quite comfortably off at the time of his separation and found no difficulty in paying for a nanny in the initial stages, and thereafter a childminder. Similarly those whose children were over ten were able to juggle their hours and maybe rely on a nearby grandparent to keep an eye on the child. Nevertheless this sort of all-demanding commitment can create enormous extra stress on the parent and might mean that they find it a struggle to progress at work.

In two cases where men had lost their jobs at the same time as their separations they both suffered all the problems traditionally associated with housewives trying to break free of the domestic routine and making satisfactory arrangements for the children. Both were seeking employment, but having adapted to the domestic role I suspect that their confidence to leave the home and children on a regular basis was in question, and probably affected their chances of landing a job.

In two further cases one would imagine that the ideal solution was readily available for they involved two qualified teachers. But this was not so. In the first case:

'As my relationship was so intense and unrelieved with my own children, I could not face the idea of working with other children.'

One can sympathise with this sentiment. In the other case the woman has not secured a permanent post:

'I don't know if my situation goes against me. I'm a relief teacher, but I've never had a permanent job. It's like an added stress.'

111

Both these women first gained employment on Manpower Services Schemes. Whereas the first was able to follow it with a permanent post the second woman was not, and she found this a further knock to her confidence:

'I had an MSC job and when that finished I was unemployed. That's when I started having counselling. I found it dreadful to have lost a job that I enjoyed so much.'

Each person's situation is unique, but in one slightly different case that I researched the partners separated eleven years ago after nineteen years of marriage. It was not based on mutual agreement, nor was it a particularly amicable separation, but neither party has taken divorce proceedings. They live entirely separately, the husband with a new partner, the wife with the two children, now nearly grown up. In this case the wife still draws 'house-keeping' from their joint account. The amount has never been reviewed, so has not kept up with the cost of living. As the years have gone by Sarah has been able to take on extra work to more or less make up the drop in value of the housekeeping. She started out as a school sandwich-watcher, keeping an eye on sixth-formers eating their lunch. (Dinner lady is one of the few jobs that really does fit in well with child-care arrangements; the big drawback of course is the low pay!) Although Sarah disliked the job she was pleased to do it, having a free cooked dinner herself plus the money earned. As her children grew older she gained employment at a library where to begin with she could work for just four hours a day, and increase them as the children grew. She was lucky to have a good friend over the road who kept an eye on the children if ever she was not there. The children called them aunt and uncle, and as their own children were growing up it suited everybody very well. Despite the fact that she has lived as a single parent for eleven years, and relations with her husband could be described only as cordial, she would still turn to him in the case of a financial crisis. When people have been married for many years before they separate, it is doubtful if all ties are ever entirely broken.

7   Your Social Life
'Normal Services Will Be Resumed as soon as Possible'

FRIENDS

Keeping Old Ones

Patterns of friendship after a separation and as a one-parent family tend to be quite different from those of a married couple or a traditional family.

Most people I spoke to socialised to some extent before the breakdown of their marriage. Quite often it seems that one or other partner was the 'leader' in forming and keeping friends, and in these cases the friends normally remained loyal to that partner:

> 'I'm friendly with people we knew. They are not friendly with him. They tended to be my friends before so have not kept contact with him.'

> 'We did not socialise much. We kept in touch with my college friends.'

> 'Our friends were mostly my friends.'

Sometimes people reported that they had managed to maintain one mutual friend, but it was never clear whether their partner remained friends with them too. The following were in answer to 'have you kept any mutual friends?':

> 'No, well one.'

> 'Possibly one. In the main, no.'

'Only one. He turned out to be a very good friend.'

The usual pattern was for the friends to keep in touch with one partner only, or to drop them both.

Sometimes couples had socialised quite heavily as a couple and only realised when they separated that they did not relate personally, but as a half of a pair. This can be one of the strengths and pleasures of a devoted couple, but it tends to back-fire in cases of divorce or widowhood:

> 'Once you come out of a relationship you suddenly realise that you can count your friends on one hand. When something like this happens they are embarrassed. They come forward with support initially, but they're acutely embarrassed. Really you've got no true friends because they are all couples.'

> 'We used to go out, occasionally to a show or something, but mostly it would be a drink. We never went out without each other. Then as things got bad, and I knew I didn't want to go anymore, that would cause a row.'

It is sad and ironic that at this time of emotional disturbance and very often isolation, people cannot turn to or rely on those they regarded as friends. Sometimes the phenomenon can be put down to embarrassment:

> 'I felt alienated at first in some situations, but I soon learnt to avoid them because I recognised that people do not want to appear partisan.'

Sometimes it is caused by the people themselves withdrawing:

> 'I just didn't want to know. I cut myself off from everybody. I felt like a leper.'

It can be very hard to approach friends after a separation. You may need their support badly, but feel you do not want to go into all the details. In the long term, people did come to rely on friends both old and new, and they tend to play a much more important part in people's lives than formerly. In the initial period, however, those who had struggled for long periods to uphold their marriage found it hard to break out of the 'couple' mould. Men seemed to suffer more than woman in this respect:

> 'I hadn't got any actual friends. They were all my ex-wife's friends.'

> 'I lost my married friends, yes. It's awkward. One or two rang up in the early days.'

> 'I was always a loner. I kept myself to myself. I'm not a mixer, although now I do.'

If you have had a network of friends try your best to keep in touch with them. Make your initial contact brief and then get in touch again fairly soon after. By this time the shock will have gone out of the news and you will find out fairly quickly if your friend wants to ostracise you. It can be extremely hurtful when people jump to conclusions or pass judgement on your behaviour without the full knowledge of what has happened:

> 'At one stage the husband of one of my friends was writing to my partner saying that they had always been grateful to him for his help and condemning me. I feel quite resentful to him for that attitude. I suppose what they had seen was the other man in my life, what they hadn't seen was the other woman in his – and she wasn't the first.'

People close to you, but not close enough to know the facts, often will be curious about what has happened. It is natural and helps them make sense of what is happening in your life and in theirs. Whenever someone reports a breakdown in a marriage it is sure to make the receiver of the information examine their own situation and reflect

116

on life's values in general. It can cause them to be very philosophical and sometimes pessimistic. Occasionally people can feel jealous that you have broken free of an unhappy relationship when they may still be trapped in one. Sometimes they are just sad at the thought of society as we know it changing. In the early days of separation when you may be shocked and emotionally raw yourself you may not be able to cope with reactions from friends. After a period of time your own emotions will subside and you should try to face people with openness and lack of resentment – it is better for your own mental health.

Good Friends

Not everything need be black on the 'friends' front. Sometimes your attitude to friends and acquaintances can affect the way that they respond to you. If you are withdrawn and sensitive they will naturally find it hard to relate to you. Sometimes it happens that desperation drives you to ask for help in some practical way – collecting the children from school or bringing in some shopping. After the initial awkwardness that barrier drops and you find in fact that you have a very good friend.

Intimate friends, and of course, lovers, are very often the prop which you lean on most at first. There is a tremendous relief involved in off-loading all the worries of the day, discussing problems and possible solutions and having things put in perspective for you by someone at least marginally more objective than you. Those people whose natures or dispositions are such that they do not have a friend to serve this purpose in the early days tend to suffer more than those who do. Two of the men who had serious breakdowns did not have anyone to fulfil this role until they were getting treatment for their condition. The treatment consisted mainly of what a lot of people, and more particularly women, do instinctively. Without the safety valve of somebody there to share your problems with, something is bound to give:

'I've never been a person to phone up and discuss
problems. I usually solve my own problems. I don't like
burdening other people with my problems, yet I'll sit
and listen for hours to other people's. I think its pride.
I'm too proud.'

'In the beginning I stayed in, never went anywhere.
Once I was back at work I would come home in the
evenings and decorate.'

Activity such as decorating can be a great therapy (*see*
Chapter 9) and there are other substitutes for companionship, but in the early days most people need and should
seek someone to talk to. If this is a major problem for you
phone Gingerbread or the Samaritans.

Most women seem to have one or two friends with
whom they could discuss things. In one case the person
was her sister. In this case the sister had been widowed at
the age of twenty seven and left with two small children.
Although the circumstances of their single parenthood
were quite different the sisters were able to give each other
tremendous support and continue to do so:

'My sister is my friend and my sister. She's my most
important friend.'

In another case a very close neighbour who had helped
out in the midst of many domestic 'emergencies' during
the stormy separation, continued to be a source of
strength and encouragement after the separation. The
physical proximity of people such as these is of terrific
value:

'My most important friend in the early days was a
neighbour. It was a relief not having to explain
everything to her when things happened.'

There is no substitute for the cup of tea or coffee to
accompany the verbal diatribe that is sometimes essential

to clear the air. Having said that, the worth of the telephone can never been over-valued.

A word of warning on the subject of leaning on friends. One should always guard against the abuse of a friend's ready ear. On the one hand you might use a particular friend so regularly to off-load that s/he becomes addicted to your out-pourings. In this case s/he may actually cease being a beneficial person to talk to. Initial commiserations and encouragement to smooth things over can, by subtle shifts, become needling remarks or less than helpful suggestions designed almost to encourage you to pursue hostilities. This may be quite unintentional and happen so gradually that neither of you is aware of it. On the other hand as you begin to recover your equilibrium and no longer feel the need to keep your friend informed of developments, s/he can feel snubbed or rejected, especially if and when a new partner appears on the scene. Always try to take an equal interest in your friend, even in your darkest moments so that your relationship does not become one-sided. Very few people are so happy themselves that they can be a continual support to someone without a bit of counter-support occasionally:

> 'I needed a lot of help, in fact I lost a friend because I needed so much help. I put it onto my one friend who had two children and difficulties herself. It broke up the friendship.'

Take good care of your friends. It is sad to lose someone who obviously cares a lot about you by over-using them.

Making New Friends

Many people expressed the satisfaction of being appreciated and liked for themselves:

> 'I enjoy the new friends I'm finding. I enjoy being liked for me.'

119

'One of the best things is getting to know people on
your own, for yourself.'

'I've got my own life now, my own friends. I'm me
now instead of part of her.'

In two cases women described how their ex-partners had
tried to prevent them from making friends. In the first
case the woman was initially quite flattered by her husband's wish to keep their relationship exclusive:

'He tried to keep me away from friends and family. I
thought it was nice at first, a sign of love for me.'

As time went on she came to the conclusion that selfishness
had a lot more to do with it:

'He hadn't got a lot of interests and he'd no friends
at all until I met him. He did not want me to continue
seeing any friends I had, the big self-centred pig.'

Another woman described how her husband had made
socialising of any sort impossible. She stopped inviting
friends into the house because he would be sarcastic to
them and all the time she would be nervous of what he'd
say. It even got to the stage where she was frightened to
tell him if she had been to her own parent's house:

'I used to have to lie. I'd take the children round and
then I'd say 'when we get back don't tell your Dad
that we've been to your Nan's'. He was jealous. I had
no friends. I never went out of the house.'

On balance people seemed to think that they enjoyed
more friendships than they did when they were one of a
couple. When you are newly separated this prospect might
seem unlikely, even impossible. It does not happen
straight away and there may be many difficult months
before you find the confidence to be yourself and make
new friends. The important thing is not to shut yourself

off, to be open, honest, friendly and approachable. Never refuse an invitation – you never know what it holds. Take a sincere interest in others and be as open-minded about them as you would like them to be about you.

You may find that your friends fall into categories. Those you make 'at the school gate' will primarily be day-time friends with children of a similar age to yours. Invite them back to your house after school – not hoards of them, or anyone who shows an unhealthy curiosity. You have a chance at the school to chat to and vet them, so take advantage of that. When you are sure that someone is genuine, invite them back. Usually you will not have the time strictures of getting a meal ready for your partner, although do not forget that they may have. You may prefer to have an 'adult' conversation with them within school hours – an hour in the morning or afternoon, and to exchange children one or two afternoons a week. It makes the evening shorter when you are on 'child duty' and gives you a break when they are.

One mother mentioned that she often offered to have other children, even keeping them overnight. But felt that she was taken advantage of. Somehow the fact that she did not have a man to 'cater' for meant that people felt that she would not mind having their children, and may even welcome their company. But they did not consider returning the favour.

On balance, if this happens, I do think that the value of the company for your children and the added warmth and activity that company brings is worth suffering the extra work and energy required. Sometimes it is pure thoughtlessness that children are not asked back, so a gentle hint – 'Would Jane like to come to my house on Tuesday and perhaps Angela can come to you next week?' – may do the trick. If it doesn't, try not to take it personally. Other people may not have the same problems as you, but they may have others that you do not know about such as awkard partners, sick parents or other commitments that keep them fully occupied.

Sometimes it happens that families are the culprits in assuming that 'poor you', deserted or abandoned, at least partnerless, need to be put upon regularly to provide them with meals or company. You can choose your friends but you cannot choose your relatives, and quite often this is not the sort of company that you need. As soon as you feel strong enough emotionally do not be afraid to state that you are sometimes busy, sometimes tired, sometimes have visitors, or are otherwise occupied. If they phone before coming do not deny them altogether, but try suggesting a postponement – it may surprise them at first. Be very careful not to be too heavy handed though, they are important to you and you would miss them if you offended them, even if you feel otherwise when they are monopolising you.

Friends at work can be a valuable source of support, or a source of annoyance. Generally speaking you can get things off your chest over a cup of coffee, and knowing that work must continue afterwards you do not become too bogged down by it. The evidence is that men on the whole do not indulge in this valuable safety valve. Not only that, in some areas of work men seem to feel that any hint of domestic problems or emotional instability might colour their promotion prospects. This is sad, but may be a justifiable fear. If colleagues are unhelpful in their atti-tude to you it can make life even more stressful. The only way to survive may be to keep a very low profile for a while.

Evening friends may be quite a different group of people, or they could be those with children who stay on after teatime. Sometimes if you find one other person in the same situation as yours it can be really quite satisfying all round to spend an afternoon and evening together. The meal is a joint one so preparation and clearing up are shared and much is gained from the feeling of 'family' generated by two adults and a larger number of children. If you get on really well this can be duplicated at weekends – Sunday dinner or a picnic in the park. It prevents you feeling isolated and different when traditional families are busy doing traditional things.

Any activity that you do with the children is probably more fun for everyone if you also do it with another adult, male or female. Sisters, cousins and aunts, beware! Extra children often help, depending on their ages and compatibility, but sometimes they can be horrifically argumentative. Another adult, however, is another person to listen and to explain to the children; and someone to chat to or share things with is an enormous help. People who in the past had either relied on their partners' friends or who never enjoyed socialising much anyway have sometimes found that they are more sociable than they realised:

> 'I never had many friends when I was with her. I've got friends now and as they are in the same situation as myself I find them easier to get on with. We talk the same language. They are easier to get on with and easier to keep.'

Sometimes leisure-time pursuits, clubs or societies have helped in this process.

SOCIALISING

The whole question of status seems to be quite a stumbling block to successful socialising, especially in group situations:

> 'Most of the people I am on good terms with are married. You feel the odd one out.'

> 'Its harder where they are all couples. You're not invited so much.'

People reported that it was much harder to make and keep friends who were couples. This was mentioned quite often. It seems to cause a mutual embarrassment so that

123

somehow everyone tries to avoid the situation arising where you are invited to a function without at least a potential partner. This can be very annoying, especially for those seeking or enjoying independence for the first time in years. If 'friends' are not trying to partner you off at every opportunity there is the other phenomenon of feeling a threat to their partners. Here is how one man described it:

> 'From what I thought were friends I was given the glass barrier syndrome. You are an outcast. I was a threat to the men. I was going to take their wives, and to the women I was a threat. I was going to jump on them and rape them. It was the last thing on my mind. They talk to you, but they keep away, sort of thing.'

and similarly from a woman:

> 'In some instances I'm conscious that I've been considered a threat – particularly as I'm very effusive at times. Men in particular regard that as an attraction to them personally, rather than an attraction to the case that I'm effusing over.'

NEW RELATIONSHIPS

Having failed once in a marriage most people feel scarred and uncertain about embarking on another. Lack of trust and cynicism were the biggest barriers at first:

> 'You think twice about making a relationship, and when you've thought twice you think another twice, and then again on top of that.'

> 'It took a long time for me to trust Adam. It took two to three years. Even now I put up barriers when I'm hurt.'

'Emotionally it would be nice to have a partner. It's
difficult now though because I put up barriers. I never
want to be hurt like that again.'

Despite these deep-seated insecurities people sometimes
fell quickly into substitute relationships without really
giving themselves time to recover from their divorces.
Their need to fill the space left by their partners seems to
override any restraint that they might exercise if they were
to be more objective. One man reported how he had
observed this at Gingerbread meetings:

'I've seen it more than once. After a few months they
get engaged. I can't believe it. There's one girl. She's
been married twice. She's been going out with this chap
for three months and she's just got engaged. I can't
believe it. She's a nice girl. She's OK.'

Several people did find new partners quite quickly after
their separation and these lasted well whilst all the proceedings were going through. It may be that quite unintentionally the newly separated person is less discriminat-
ing than otherwise because they are so thankful to have
someone to support them through their difficult times:

'I went out with David for about eighteen months. I was
able to share things with him. It helped when things
were going through the solicitor. But it foundered soon
after everything had gone through. I think he felt
used.'

It could be that having come through the most traumatic
stages of the proceedings and still surviving people
actually felt better about themselves and perhaps, therefore, in a position to be more selective. This was borne out
by another mother:

'The relationship I had during the proceedings raised
my self-worth. I have become more self-confident.'

125

In other cases people grasped at a new opportunity because it seemed to offer something that had been missing in their marriages:

> 'I had a brief relationship when I left my husband. It was a 'grasping at straws' situation. He appeared very glamorous to me. I was so dragged down that I needed a bit of sparkle. He proved not to be glamorous or particularly sparkling. It was disastrous as a relationship. He was not what I thought him to be. He made me very, very wary.'

> 'I slipped into an easy sort of relationship which seemed to have all the caring lacking in my marriage – but I came to realise that that was not enough.'

In other cases, where a marriage had ended because of a new partner, the relationships survived at the time of writing for up to ten years.

If those deserted by their spouse did not immediately find a substitute, and in those cases where the immediate substitute was discarded, there usually followed a fairly substantial period without a replacement. Initially people were often too numb and shocked to even consider a new relationship. Apart from the practical problems of getting out to meet new people, the children can create difficulties which make you feel it just is not worth it. They can be very resentful of a newcomer to the home, even on a very platonic basis, and children normally polite and well-mannered to visitors can be disturbingly rude and contradictory if they feel threatened by someone you seem to like. People get over this in various ways, but mainly, unless they are very sure that their new partner is going to be permanent, they defer to the children and keep their new friend in the background.

> 'The two boys resent her. They get on all right talking to her, but I could never have a relationship at home. I think they lose respect for you. I'll have to wait until the kids leave home.'

'I do find my daughter limits my social behaviour. I could never invite anybody back to stay, but I've come to terms with that. My social life has expanded rather than the reverse, although it is not necessarily home-based.'

As these parents both have teenage children moral values and behaviour are fairly high in their thoughts anyway. Most parents still wish their children to observe the fundamental morals of sex only within a committed and permanent relationship, even if they themselves have slipped upon the moral tightrope. There may have been a tendency since the advent of modern contraception for lone parents to seek solace and comfort in sometimes flippant and gratuitous sexual relationships. The dangers of modern diseases may mean that lone parents will now be forced to develop far better social relationships before entering into sexual ones and that these solid foundations will give relationships a better chance of surviving.

People with younger children usually fare slightly better with new partners. Up to a certain age young children seem fairly open-minded about newcomers and quite willing to welcome them. They are only interested in the sleeping arrangements from a practical point of view, though parents naturally will protect them from embarrassment. Even so, the new partner can find it very hard to adopt a role within the family especially if the children see a lot of both their parents.

After a period of time as a lone parent, women in particular seem to reach the stage where they have almost become too self-sufficient to need anyone else. They actually begin to enjoy their condition. Whilst this is a healthy and positive attitude to have about oneself, it can be a handicap when it comes to working at new relationships:

'I don't really feel a practical need for a partner. Emotionally it would be nice but it can create difficulties

127

because I'm self-sufficient. It annoys me now when someone tries to help me and I know I can do it.'

In a sense, once one is established as a single parent, it gets easier to remain that way, and you have to think hard about what you want out of a new relationship. Quite often people become harder to please and more selective once they have proved to themselves that they can manage alone anyway:

'I did have a relationship, but when my son asked me if we were going to move I said it hadn't gone that far. It made me think what I wanted out of a relationship. I knew I didn't want marriage, even though I liked her.'

Even when people have found partners whom they are happy to accept as permanent replacements there can be problems if the new partners have children of their own to accommodate. Very often a rather bizarre kaleidoscope of relationships develops, constantly shifting and changing, sometimes more stable than others. It can take years before things finally settle into any sort of regular pattern.

Practically everybody I spoke to, encompassing people separated for anything from between twelve months and twelve years, had found a new partner at some stage. People found their partners in a variety of ways, most commonly at their place of work.

SINGLES CLUBS AND MAGAZINES

Those who had sampled clubs for divorced and separated people seemed to gain the impression that they were not the best places to go to meet people for a permanent relationship. They may be a good place to go for a night out, to have a drink and to meet people on a very superficial level. Some people, however, made a habit of frequenting the 'singles' clubs, and got to know others on 'the circuit' quite well!

Two people I spoke to had used and highly recommend the magazine *Singles*. This is a monthly magazine where people who want to meet others, and in particular a partner, advertise themselves. The first person, a woman, recommended the magazine because she felt so safe doing it. You have a box number so cannot be reached directly, and the progress of events is controlled by you. She described how she had waited years thinking that men were not interested in her, but in fact she was delighted by the many marvellous replies she had to her advert. She liked the positive feeling that she gained from knowing that the men were looking for a serious relationship, and was able to be quite specific about her tastes in the advert. In fact this lady met someone very suitable straight away and was somewhat disappointed that she was unable to pursue some of the others who had introduced themselves.

Here is an account of the second person's experience, in this case a man:

'I didn't want to be isolated. I wanted a partner. I wrote off for the magazine and on receiving it I wrote letters to five. Not one replied, which upset me a bit. Then I placed an advert myself. In the first week I received one reply, and thought it was a waste of money. By the end of the month I'd received sixty-two replies. The only drawback is that none of them were local. They were from all over the country. From the *Singles* magazine I now have three people that I see on a girlfriend/boyfriend basis – we go out occasionally. It's nice. It's company. I recommend it.'

Meeting a partner in our society is often difficult anyway, but when you have children it can be harder still. This is one way of finding someone from your armchair! Many people feel that they are above this sort of deliberate matchmaking, that fate and romance should direct their love lives. It is better to do something positive like this and

129

meet new and interesting people than to exist alone because no one has 'found' you. The address of 'Singles' is 23 Abingdon Road, London, W8 6AH (telephone 01 938 1011).

8 Day by Day

In this chapter I first examine the sadder and more negative side of being a lone parent. This is partly to indicate to those who are undecided about whether or not they should separate, the true and long-term difficulties that they may have to face, and partly to demonstrate the same to any professionals who may be trying to understand the problems of one-parent families. As an antidote I would recommend the last section of the chapter on the positive aspects of being a single parent, and the next chapter, on therapies!

LONELINESS AND ISOLATION

Isolation and loneliness are probably the worst aspects of being a lone parent. Bearing sole responsibility full time runs a close second. People felt and expressed their isolation or loneliness in different ways.

For some people suddenly being one alone instead of one of a couple was the hardest thing about it. One man, when asked all the questions about missing the little things answered quietly 'no' to each of them:

'No, I miss somebody else.'

'No, I just miss somebody else.'

Even when the decision to separate has been your own, the loneliness and despair that follows can be desperate, and the wish to be part of a couple can still be strong. The sight of other couples spending time together can sometimes cause distress. It can put you in a very reflective mood and emphasise the loneliness of your situation. This seemed to most affect those who used to share household chores with their partners:

> 'We always went shopping together. Looking at other couples I used to think, why can't that be us?.'

Other people found the sight of happy families on the television upsetting, or the portrayal of a wedding scene would bring them to tears. None of us escape these experiences without trauma and these sensitivities and scars can last for years. On the other hand sometimes people become their own worst enemies and hinder a healthy recovery. Others still viewed 'happy couples' from a rather different perspective:

> 'Sometimes I have slight envy when I see couples together, but I know that the real experience doesn't match the reality.'

> 'No, I don't mind seeing couples shopping. When I see them arguing I have a good laugh. It gives me a sense of freedom.'

Holidays sometimes brought out the most romantic or sentimental responses:

> 'Again you are isolated. You walk over the beach, enjoying the atmosphere, but you see lots of couples frolicking in the sands or having meals together, and you do miss that very much.'

Then again, there were those who are rather more down to earth:

> 'I only notice couples on holiday, but I deliberately look at the husbands and usually I think I'm better off without that!'

If you are alone when you would rather be one of a couple it can be sad and depressing, but do not allow yourself to wallow in the state unrealistically. Enjoy your singleness for what it is. There is every chance that you will meet someone and become part of a couple again in the future. So make the most of your individuality for the present.

SUICIDE FANTASIES AND PANIC ATTACKS

The constant loneliness and stress of coping day after day without the release of someone to share one's problems with can build up into a desperate situation. Several people mentioned that they had thought of suicide:

'I eventually got to the stage where I did not feel the children were enough to live for. I just wanted someone to love. I took all my iron tablets, but they just gave me diarrhoea.'

'I felt loneliest at night-time when the kids were in bed. I used to count the patterns on the wallpaper. I'd sometimes walk miles with the kids in the pushchair. I once thought of putting all three of us under a bus.'

Perhaps I should mention that both these people have found new partners, and so far as one can judge, are now content. One elaborated on how she often has suicide fantasies, although she is sure she would never carry them out:

'It's extraordinary the things you think of. Last winter I had a fantasy of pouring petrol over myself and setting fire to myself. I had never had that one before. Usually it's sort of throwing yourself out of a window.'

This woman felt particularly affected by the long winter evenings, when, without transport, she would feel trapped in her house once darkness had fallen. Other things that would trigger fantasies are bad weather, financial worries or stress at work. This may sound rather dramatic to those who have never experienced such feelings, but I suspect that many more people in the lone parent situation suffer this sort of depression than admit it. Several people described situations where they felt deeply depressed or suddenly panicked. It can be very frightening and cause strange and bizarre behaviour to find yourself alone at night at a time when you suddenly feel totally unable to cope. Knowing that you are not going mad but having a normal reaction to excessive stress can be a relief in itself. It's best to phone someone straight away, and if they can come round, so much the better. If there is no one you know personally who can fulfill this role, then ring the Samaritans. They are only a phone call away and waiting to help in such situations.

Several people mentioned having to argue with themselves, or talk themselves out of such black moods. Do this on paper if possible. It makes you think more rationally and is a form of distraction. (*See* Chapter 9 on therapies for other tips.) In the end the passage of time and your own will-power play a large part in your recovery:

'I had to fight depression. I would sit down and lecture myself. I would tell myself that I had to go and be active. Activity in itself is a therapy. I thought it was a black tunnel, with no light at the end, but I have come through it. I reminded myself that I was happy in love once, and that it came to an end. It was cynical but true. In the end I came to terms with loneliness on my own. It was far easier to bear than the loneliness in my marriage.'

BEARING SOLE RESPONSIBILITY

After loneliness, the worst thing about being a single parent is often the total and unrelieved responsibility for everything. The fear of illness is particularly strong in those caring for young children. It is often difficult to have an off day even if there are two parents. When you are the only one, it is impossible, although the stresses and strains you have to bear may make you far more vulnerable than you would otherwise be. This is another reason why sharing the care successfully with your ex-partner can be so important. Where this is not posssible share your concerns with others and seek help when you need it. Do not try to survive alone.

THE HOUSEHOLD

Domestic chores can sometimes actually be lighter than before, especially if yours was the sort of partner who never lifted a finger anyway. As one woman said:

> 'Housework is a lot easier. It's like having a big baby removed.'

There were several women who voiced similar sentiments; that their husbands never helped about the house anyway and that now they had the freedom to regulate the household to suit themselves, rather than having to revolve around their husbands' needs.

The story from men coping alone was similar. Without exception they claimed that they were the ones to do most of the household chores anyway. This was not voiced in any martyred sense. In the main they were not critical of their wives contribution to the chores:

> 'I didn't miss any of that because I did most of it anyway – but she was a good housewife, she was an excellent housewife.'

It was usually just the way that things had evolved, perhaps through working shifts, from both working, or from natural preferences. The men left to care for the children had plenty of practical experience. Here is a sample of their comments:

'I was brought up to be able to cope. My mother was a
cripple. I love cooking, especially baking cakes, and I've
brought up the children to do that. I did the housework.
I did the cooking. I was already doing that.'

'I could cook and keep tidy anyway. Washing, ironing,
all that. I'd had a lot of practice before – she used to go
out a lot.'

In fact the answers in this respect were so similar that one
did wonder if men competent at household chores run the
risk of undermining the confidence of their partners. One
of the women expressed such a feeling about her husband.
True, she had just returned from hospital and the husband was trying to be helpful, but although society often
calls for equality and an end to sexism, not everybody is
equipped to handle it in practice:

'He took over in the house and did everything. He
made me redundant. I felt a stranger in my own
house.'

Only one of the men expressed any qualms about his
ability to keep house, and that only fleetingly:

'One thing I still cannot handle is cooking. Housework
and ironing I can do. The only thing I find hard is
cooking and that will come with time.'

As far as the more traditional 'male' tasks were concerned, none of the men expressed any difficulties and
most of the women were willing and even eager to develop
new skills:

'My son helps me practically, but I want to learn things,
because he used to do all that. I'm trying to do things
myself, even though they look a mess. I'm learning.'

'I've always been very proficient in doing things. I'm
very handy. I didn't do any decorating till after I

136

became a single parent, but I've always been good at
doing things so there was no hardship in it.'

Sometimes this proficiency can create problems if and
when a new partner is found. Men were reported to be
very poor at allowing or enabling women to do practical
things for themselves, although one woman who has been
a single parent for many years was proud of the male
contacts she had made who did just that:

'I've developed one or two men friends who will help
with jobs by letting me do as much as I can myself.'

For instance she would do the painting and her friend do
the papering, thus minimising the cost and giving her
some satisfaction in what she had achieved. Of course, this
sort of division of labour can be applied to many tasks, and
in an ideal world would be, to suit people's individual
skills and preferences.

There is no doubt that not having a partner to cater for
allows you much more flexibility in running the household. Make sure that you take advantage of this rather
than dwelling on the negative or lonely aspects. You can
cook and eat what you want, when you want; obviously you
take account of the children's needs, but they will usually
fall in quite happily with your wishes in this respect. Some
people found this hard to adapt to. Although they enjoyed
many aspects of not having a partner to have to wait on,
they could not get used to being able to please themselves:

'I miss not having someone to make the tea for. I feel
guilty at making something for myself without including
him. At first I could not make things for myself.'

'I used to miss sitting down and eating a meal together,
knowing that I had prepared it. I felt appreciated in a
way children cannot show.'

137

Traditional roles and routines go haywire in the one-parent situation. The best way to deal with this is to try to gain the benefits of both. Enjoy your control over what you do when, but retain those elements of traditional family life that still help you and the children. As one man pointed out, there is a danger that you can spend so much time working in one sense or another that you do not actually give enough time to playing with the children. It is extremely demanding on you, but if you are trying to fulfil the role of both parents most of the time, it is very important that you do.

Every working parent knows this is a constant problem and energy is not always forthcoming when it would be welcomed. Having a traditional family meal once a week can be a focal point for relaxing and then spending time together. If you spend all week rushing around, eating and feeding on demand try to have one meal at the weekend when you always sit together to a proper meal, and do something together afterwards. There is a danger that if we never conform to traditions such as 'Sunday dinner', we miss the opportunity of bonding the family unit together. Eating together, conversing together and then playing – board games, swimming, walking and so on, can be an important focal point in an otherwise topsy-turvy existence.

THE LITTLE THINGS

Despite the compensations of being able to please yourself more often, there are undoubtedly many little things that will be difficult day to day and that will take some getting used to. One of the little things that I missed, and still do, is being brought a cup of tea in bed in the morning. Many a marriage has survived long and strong without either partner benefiting from such a ritual, but undoubtedly it is something that one partner often does for the other and a simple act that can be significantly missed. People

138

overcame this particular problem in a variety of ways. Often they would say that the children would bring them a cup of tea in bed from quite a young age, even when their partners had not. In two cases people bought themselves a teasmaid to solve the problem:

'I bought a teasmaid. When I told him I could see him thinking 'That's all she wanted me for!'

As children get older they were often able to make tea and meals proficiently at a comparatively young age. However, in general the tendency to make the same for their lone parent wore off with the novelty!

The sound of the key in the door is something else that can be very evocative. When you are alone with the children all day the sound of the key in the lock can raise your spirits and morale immeasurably. It marks the end of a long and tiring day without any adult conversation or stimulation. Much as you may love and enjoy your children that point when the key goes in the lock is a signal that the sole responsibility for them is over for another day. For many lone parents this never comes, and the continuing responsibility for household and children is hard to bear.

For other parents I talked to, the sound often had an ambivalent meaning to them. Several people, when asked if they miss the sound of the key in the door, changed their initial reply:

'No, but in a way, yes.'

'Yes, to know you're not alone; but no sometimes, because I was safe. The bad part had gone.'

Some people did not miss the sound at all. Their children may have keys, or their partners' comings and goings were very erratic anyway, and for several it was a relief to know that they would no longer hear that sound:

139

'He kept odd hours anyway. The separation was very gradual. I never knew when he was going to come in the door. Mixture really, more relief.'

'I used to dread the sound of the key in the door. It's a relief not to hear it now.'

Conversely, coming into an empty house can be a new and upsetting experience for many, especially if, for instance, the children are staying at your partner's. You may be on your own for the first time for ages:

'It doesn't worry me now, but I didn't like it at first. It would be really quiet. I used to be a bit nervous.'

'I hated this. I could actually feel the emptiness and the silence.'

'I hate coming home to empty silence. I now leave the radio on so it's not so quiet on my return. It helps a little.'

Leaving the radio on is a solution that several people mentioned, and, of course, leaving a light on if it's going to be dark on your return helps a bit too. The physical temperature of the house can make a big difference too. If you are working at making the atmosphere 'right' for you and the children, try to arrange it that the house is always warm and cosy when you come in. Of course this is not always possible, but a blow-heater works very quickly and there is no doubt that the sound of a radio or television makes the place feel lived in as opposed to deserted. Pets can make a difference in this respect, especially the ready welcome of a dog.

PETS

Pets can be a tremendous asset. They can be companions, toys and teaching aids. Children gain much from loving and caring for another living creature. It helps them develop a sense of responsibility towards others and themselves. Pets also give a home warmth and atmosphere. Small caged animals are fairly cheap, but should not be regarded as dispensable. They do have a tendency to die unless they are carefully selected and cared for. Make sure you do your homework on the care of one of these little creatures before buying one. Those that do survive become treasured members of the household. Larger pets are of course more expensive to keep, but repay this in full in the love and loyalty that they give. One mother summed it up as follows:

'Pets are extremely important, from a loving point of view, but also (unfortunately) from a position of domination or fantasy. If I've been cross with Lisa she might fantasise her anger or frustration through the pets. They are also baby substitutes and friends – but she knows how to respect and love animals.'

PHOTOGRAPHS

Some families take many photos, others few. This is a delicate subject because photos can be powerfully evocative, and generate strong feelings of anger, bitterness, remorse and sadness. There can be a temptation to part with all such reminders of the past in an attempt to dissociate yourself from your former life. At first it is extremely hard and probably not advisable to look at photos of the past, of happier times or of those no longer a part of your life. Nevertheless, all children enjoy photos of their history and they at least are entitled to look at them. After all, photos are usually a glimpse of the happy times and remembering them may help. You may find that the first time you look at your wedding or other such photos it upsets you. One way to overcome this is to look through them with a friend. Later look through them again, with another friend if possible, and later still look through

141

them on your own. With any luck you will find that you have somehow dealt with that part of your history and put it into perspective. After this it should be easier to spend an odd occasion with the children looking at and enjoying bits of their past.

HOLIDAYS

Holidays should be a relaxing time when you and the children unwind from all the rush and cares of the year. It is well documented that family holidays often produce more stress than relaxation, and in the single-parent situation this can be even worse.

The pressure on all of you to enjoy this well-earned and eagerly anticipated break can make it very hard actually to relax when the time finally comes. Being a lone parent amongst masses of holidaying families can accentuate your situation and your loneliness. Men taking daughters find that they get strange looks from fellow holidaymakers and women alone feel they have to keep a low profile lest they attract too much attention to their situation. I think the best solution is to go in a group, with individual and private accommodation so that you can all escape each other some of the time. Friends or family might fit the bill, or perhaps a Gingerbread holiday might suit you (*see* Chapter 10).

Do not be tempted to take along a newly acquired partner. It might seem like a good idea to you, but to your children this is an intruder come to steal your precious attention just when they were hoping to enjoy most of it. Tears, tantrums and bad behaviour are bad enough at home, but they are even worse on holiday, without the normal recourses to discipline, especially if you are trying to impress someone. Better to save new relationship holidays for another time, perhaps a weekend away when the children are somewhere else. Use the opportunity of the family holiday to spend lots of time playing with and talking to your offspring without begrudging them the attention they deserve.

CHRISTMAS, NEW YEAR, BIRTHDAYS AND ANNIVERSARIES

These are all bound to cause you some reflection on how things used to be. New Year in particular seems to be the loneliest time, when people report being in company but feeling alone. One person's solution to this is simply not to celebrate New Year and she has felt much better since ignoring it. If you are celebrating New Year, try not to dwell on what the past has been, but think positively about the future and the new opportunities you have to develop yourself.

Several people found that Christmas can be better than before. Sometimes partners had regimented Christmas, or refused to socialise with the rest of the family, and in these cases separated parents find a new pleasure at this time. They can relax as they wish and several people joined together with their extended families to have a big celebration that they and their children really enjoy and which they could never do before. The most important thing seems to be to avoid trying to do the same as when you were a two-parent family. It can never be the same, and it can trigger a series of unhappy and unhelpful moods. Do something different, go somewhere different, and have fun.

For children's birthdays invite along plenty of adult helpers so that the second parent is not missed. Children quite often enjoy a double celebration so they may not feel hard done by. On your own birthday treat yourself to something which you really want. It is sad that there is no one to do it for you, but at least you will get something which you know you will like, so count that as a bonus. There seems to be no solution to the reminders that come on anniversaries, except, perhaps, the passage of time.

SOME POSITIVE ASPECTS OF SINGLE PARENTHOOD

Despite the months and sometimes years of turbulence and trauma experienced by couples that separate, many people finally emerge more content, more relaxed, having gained in strength, and feeling pride in themselves. Where the partners disappeared early in children's lives the parents felt pleased that they had been able to bring them up without conflict or interference. They had confidence in their own abilities as parents and felt that they enjoyed strong but healthy relationships with their children.

For those who suffered a divorce during their children's formative years there is no doubt that they feel regret and sadness at the hurt that their children must suffer. In some cases this has led to a permanent and heartbreaking rift between parent and child. In those cases where the relationship has recovered from this knock the parent and child are seen to enjoy a close and often improved relationship with both parents, though separated. Parents themselves can often grow to enjoy their single state, and whilst they may face hardships, they also find compensations and even advantages in their life-style. Here parents speak for themselves about the positive side of being alone:

> 'We're happier in ourselves, closer to each other. I've gained friends because I never had any before. I get out more. It's a relief and a freedom to go out and enjoy it' – a mother with sole custody of six children, separated for four years.

> 'I've learnt how to be more responsible and how to be independent. What I've done I've done on my own. I'm more jolly. Mum and the neighbours have remarked on the change' – a mother with sole custody of two children, separated for four years.

> 'I've been able to bring up Matthew without any interference. It has strengthened me as a person. I am

144

more competent in many areas' – a mother with sole custody of a son, separated for ten years.

'I feel I've been allowed another crack at life. I've found laughter. I enjoy my independence. Your independence comes back and you realise that you're quite a strong character. You find your own identity' – a father with joint custody of a son, separated for one year.

'I'm more honest with myself, and in my role as a mother. I explain myself more, feel more accountable. I like to view things as a challenge, as another thing to overcome. Even the paying of the bills is satisfying. I'm pleased that I can look after myself. People say I've changed, but I haven't. I've reverted to my personality before the crisis. There are no pressures on me' – a mother with joint custody of a daughter, separated for five years.

'I'm much more independent, as everyone should be. As a partner you hide behind other people deliberately. As a single parent you have to do things yourself. People should be able to cope with the single state. We're all single at some stage. I've enjoyed getting to know people for myself, and all the things I can do without consulting anyone. When I was married I had to apologise on holiday if it rained' – a mother with joint custody of two children, separated for eleven years.

'You do grow to like it. You get a sense of achievement out of it because you've got complete control over the upbringing of the child. It's a sort of freedom. I feel quite proud of being a single parent and I feel very positive about single parenting. I also speak out in favour of it. I don't see it as a problem' – a mother with sole custody of a daughter, separated for ten years.

9 Therapies

COUNSELLING

Counselling is a structured form of therapy. I only met one woman who had had regular counselling, although some of the men had received it as part of their treatment for mental breakdowns. They all found it of great value. Other people expressed the need or wish for it, but had not actually sought it. Some people are already getting counselling from their own circle of friends or relatives, and when this is the case they often gain as much from these people who thoroughly understand the situation as from somebody objective trying to help.

There are various ways that you can come by counselling if you feel you want it. You can ask your doctor to refer you – there may be a counsellor who has sessions at his surgery, or at the local health centre. You can ask at the Citizens' Advice Bureau whether there are any local groups who do crisis or relationship counselling. Of course the marriage guidance service, now called 'Relate' aims to counsel people with relationship problems, and if you want help with the reorganisation of the family then the Family Conciliation Service, if there is one near to you, are the people to contact. Gingerbread gives a form of counselling in its meetings or telephone helplines, as do the Samaritans in a crisis situation, and both may refer you to another organisation subsequently. The National Council for One-Parent Families will be able to send you detailed information of help groups and counselling services in your area. Here is one person's comments on the value of counselling:

'It helps me to have someone to talk to because it's easy for me to get things out of proportion. I asked my

doctor to refer me. That was crisis counselling. Earlier
this year I went for some in-depth counselling. I pay her.
I need someone to talk to. Basically it puts things in
perspective.'

DISTRACTIONS

Sometimes the only therapy needed is something to take
your mind off the situation, perhaps another interest,
another occupation, or another activity. This can be in
larger or smaller forms. Sometimes part-time employment
or an evening class can fit the bill. It relieves the continuing struggle against loneliness and introspection. Sometimes the distraction has to be smaller and more
immediate than this. The fundamental solution is often
activity – of any sort.

Telephoning

Practically all the women that I spoke to regarded the
telephone as their life-line:

'When I've been low or tearful I would phone my
sister-in-law, or a friend, and they've talked me through
it.'

Whatever else you cannot manage to afford, do try to keep
your phone. It can be your contact with reality, and a
source of strength and support in times of difficulty.
When you feel caged in because the children are in bed, or
the weather is bad, or it is after dark and you have no
transport to get out and about, your phone will still be
available. Obviously the biggest drawback is that of building up a huge bill. People find different ways round this.
Always use the off-peak times to make routine phone-calls
that can wait. Even if you are feeling bad and in need of
communication try in the first instance to wait until the
cheaper times. Sometimes this will work in your favour

because in the meantime you may find another therapy that solves the problem and removes the need for the phone-call.

If you have regular lengthy chats with particular friends, and these can be extremely helpful, come to some arrangement whereby after fifteen minutes you replace the receiver and reverse the direction of the call, so that you are effectively 'going halves'. If your friend is in better circumstances than you she may offer to ring you back more often than you can ring her. Other ways of economising can be to use an egg-timer or oven-timer to remind you of the time. It might even be worth investing in one to leave permanently by the phone – especially if you have teenagers. Set it as soon as you get through and tell your friend about it so that you can ring off amicably when the bell or buzzer goes. You may find that you ignore the sound when it does come, but it's worth a try, and it will also ensure that you do not monopolise other people when they may have other things to do. Better to leave them in suspense and wanting to phone you again than boring them to bits so that they cringe next time you ring.

Encourage other people to ring you. The sound of the telephone ringing on a dark depressing night can really raise one's spirits. Try to be bright and responsive even when you are low. You can still say how you feel, you do not have to live a lie. State your feelings, but have consideration for theirs too – if you are always deathly gloomy they will find it harder and harder to bring themselves to call you. And remember to say 'thanks for listening' at the end of a call.

Writing Things Down

This is a therapy which may not suit everyone, but which I believe would benefit many people who have not tried it. People often speak of arguing things out in their heads – talking themselves round or going over past conversations

– trying to work things out in order to come to some solution. Writing things on paper can help you to get one stage further along the line, either to develop your argument, to see things more clearly, or just to get them off your chest. Buy a cheap note-pad and keep it with a pen in a handy place. Use it at any or every opportunity, just to make expletives if you wish, when you cannot shout out loud because of the children. More seriously, if you make a habit of jotting down things that have happened – how you feel, what you hope for each night when the children are in bed, it can have a wonderful purging effect on your brain, and allow you some peaceful sleep uncluttered with all the points that you have spilled out on paper. Write as you think and as you feel – let it flow. No one else need ever see it, although it can be very interesting reading for yourself in the future. You can compare your hopes with your achievements. If it is anger and emotion that you have put down on paper you may find that screwing it up and throwing it away afterwards helps in some strange way to deal with it.

Yoga

Several people mentioned how beneficial they had found yoga. Having talked to those who have practised it, and having read a little about it, it seems that it is a method of uncluttering the mind, of purifying body and soul, and enabling one to face life with renewed strength.

There are several forms of yoga. You do not have to go for the deeply meditational or strongly contortionist types. Those I spoke to have found the form that suits them. One prefers to do exercises alone for twenty minutes each night, another likes to join in a class where she benefits also from the companionship of others. You may like to get a book from the library in the first instance, or to join an adult education class in school hours or in the evenings if you are able to get out. The beauty of yoga is that it not only helps you mentally, but it tones and improves your body, each in turn helping the other. In one case I researched it had incidentally brought about a halt to the escalation of bedtime drinking:

> 'I was knocking myself out each night, but since I took up yoga I've become more aware of the chemical changes that were taking place when I had a drink and I didn't like them. I started to actually dislike the chemical changes so I've more or less given up drinking.'

Walking

Many people have found walking a great help. Collectively, lonely and unhappy people must have walked thousands of miles. In a way they are either walking away from their problems or walking towards other people and company.

Whatever the weather and whilst your children are small enough to wrap up well and put in a pushchair, you can resort to walking, although obviously not after dark. During daylight hours you can get out with the children for a long or a short walk. Make it brisk and business-like to revitalise yourself. A brisk walk around the block can change the mood of everyone. If you and your child are getting each other down, get those coats on and go for a walk. With little ones you can go to the park, to feed the ducks or have a swing. If you prefer to be near other people go window shopping in the town. You do not have to stay out long – the children may not allow you to anyway – but it can unaccountably brighten your spirits. Older children may be resistant to this sort of activity, although a dog can provide the perfect excuse, if you have one. If not you can still go walking when the children are at school, or staying with other people. Set off briskly and keep it up for as long as you can. Without the children you can grab a swing in a deserted park and swing yourself to oblivion and back again. If nothing else, the physical activity and fresh air does you good, sharpens your appetite and aids sleep.

150

Swimming

A good all-round toner, this is something you can do with children of all ages, all year round. It can be expensive these days, but choose the less luxurious pools which are often warm and uncrowded, and try to make it a weekly event that is included in your budget. If possible spend some time relaxing on your back, and some time trying a bit of serious swimming. If you go with a friend you can take it in turns to mind the children. Exert yourself physically as much as possible and have a warm shower afterwards to relax you, and to get your money's worth!

Keeping Fit

Keep-fit activities are a splendid way to get you out of yourself. They combine a change of scene and company with the added bonus of making yourself fitter and healthier. The best way to do them is at a small local club where you are likely to meet people who live nearby and who may thus become friends in their own right. Socialising amongst adult company can be marvellous after being locked into children's conversations and household chores all day. Badminton has the advantage of attracting both sexes, which usually means that everyone is a little better behaved – a little more courteous and considerate than in single-sex activities. If you are unable to get to a class for one reason or another, borrow a keep-fit tape from the library, or a friend, to do at home. You will not have the bonus of the company, but it can still be fun, and you can do it with the children if they are so inclined.

If this sort of structured exercise does not suit you simply do your own thing when your mood demands it. Put the radio on and fling your arms about, jump up and down, and generally let it all hang out! If it appeals to you, twist and shout! You can have great fun once the children are in bed doing improvised dance and movement. There is no one to see you so take advantage of the situation to dance, stretch, and, if your sound-proofing allows, yelp! We are such an inhibited nationality that it may be hard at first, but if nothing else, the giggles that you dissolve into will be a therapy in themselves.

Singing

A much neglected and under-valued therapy, singing is something that we all can and should do. If your children are little you have a wonderful excuse. Teach them as many nursery rhymes and children's songs as you can remember, and sing them often. If you cannot remember many, for a very small outlay, there are some excellent tapes in the shops today of children singing, or simply get a song-book from the library. Once you have learnt some of them by heart songs are a wonderful occupation during boring things like car journeys, in waiting rooms, or at bus-stops, and can prevent both you and the children becoming fractious. You may feel a bit silly in some situations, but most people will smile and enjoy the spectacle of you and your children singing. Surely this is far preferable to the black frowns that inevitably surround us if we should dare to lose patience with our child!

Singing for your own pleasure in the evening can be very enjoyable too. Get some song-books from the library and sing songs from your favourite musicals, or songs that you learnt at school. Sing them gustily and get the cobwebs out of your vocal cords. If you were taught the recorder at school see if you can borrow one, or use your child's, or even buy one. Play the tunes through first and then sing them out loud. Put expression into the songs – it will help you unlock your emotions so that you do not remain trapped in a deeply depressed mood.

Smiling

Smiling is infectious, and furthermore it is almost impossible to be angry or morose with a smile on your face. I recommend an inane grin at every opportunity – doing the washing up, making the beds, cleaning the toilet. It seems daft at first, but if you persevere and try to keep that smile up for as long as possible and as often as possible, it really can convert your mood and your outlook. In particular you should exercise your gift of smiling – not inanely, but friendly and welcoming – when approaching or meeting other people. There can be this terrible tendency to lower your chin, mouth and eyes, so that as far as they can see, you have not the least interest in them.

I was a solitary child in many ways and one of the games I used to love to play was trying to make strangers smile at me. I used to walk miles each Friday evening to my piano lessons and as I ran and skipped along I would look smilingly into the homecoming commuters' faces and grin at them stupidly. It never ceased to amaze me how readily people's tired and serious faces transformed into rays of sunshine at the sight of this impudent little child bouncing fun and sparkle at them. Do not be put off at the first hurdle. It may not always work. Sometimes others cannot be persuaded to play the smiling game, but do persevere. Eventually you will find that you have a genuine smile on your face, and the accompanying mood to go with it, far more often than you used to.

Home-Making

Often people reported that they would have to 'keep on the go' around the house. Those people are probably the ones who need to learn to relax, to let the occasional chore go unheeded, to treat themselves to a convenience meal, or a luxurious bath, or a box of chocolates in front of the fire, with restful music playing or a good book to hand. However, those people who tend to let housework slide and who have lost interest in the home and appearances, would benefit considerably from the occasional housework bonanza. Make your mind up to get the house straight. If necessary pretend that someone whom you really like, or really fear, is coming on a visit. It's amazing how quickly things can be set to rights if you put your mind to it. You may even feel less tired after you have tidied, washed up and put the clothes away than you did before, when you retreated into a sort of sluggish inertia. Try to keep on top of household chores. If necessary bribe yourself with rewards – an evening out, a friend to visit or a new household item for the kitchen (proper tools for the job make life easier) – providing that the house is clean and tidy.

Similarly with decoration. Obviously finances play a much greater part in the plan of things in this case, but careful budgeting is the key to many of the positives in your situation. You may not be able to furnish and decorate the house as you would ideally wish, but do aim to keep it as homely and as welcoming as possible. A change of curtains can change the whole atmosphere in a room, and a few pictures or a lamp can transform it from clinical and cold to warm and homely. True, even these 'small' items can be alarmingly expensive, but if and when you do get a windfall, or are able to save, be sensible in your spending so that you get items that would otherwise be out of your reach, but which are so worthwhile because they affect you and your family every day.

Conversely with clutter, if one is hard up there is a danger that you not only become the local charity case, but you actually encourage this situation by gladly accepting any bit of junk that comes your way. I do not mean that cruelly. Many people will have had a situation saved by the kind and timely donation of a much needed item of furniture, but the ongoing collection of such items after the need has passed can lead to an unseemly mess which is difficult to keep clean and which gives you little motivation to do so. Perfect the art of declining 'gifts' gracefully. 'No thanks. My lounge is now complete,' or something along those lines will suffice. It can be tricky, especially if your lounge is rather obviously not complete, but your home is a reflection of you, your family and your life-style.

Re-establishing your home in your own taste is an important aid to your healthy recovery.

Handicrafts

At a time when your brain is buzzing with questions and answers, and all your bodily functions are working overtime with worry and stress, doing something relaxing with your hands can be very therapeutic. If you knit, now is the time to get your easy patterns out and to take advantage of your state of mind to click away whenever you have a spare moment. In a way this sort of activity concentrates the mind, which may not always be what you want – sometimes you may prefer a distraction – but at other times this constructive use of nervous energy can help to soak up all the unnecessary vibrations you are giving off, so that you can quietly think your way through the maze in your mind.

Think back to handicrafts that you enjoyed as a child. Tapestry or cross-stitch pictures can be very satisfying, and you have an end result to be proud of, as well as a constructive use of your spare time. One person I spoke to had taken advantage of his situation to make himself a four-poster bed, something that he had always wanted, hand-carved and beautifully made. If your spirits or finances do not allow such elaborate or expensive pursuits there are others that cost very little. Activities such as jigsaws, which can be left out so that you put in a piece each time you pass it, or colouring in, usually ignored as childish, but in fact very therapeutic. Try to view these simple activities positively. They may well aid your mental health at a time when other opportunities are not there.

Assertiveness Training

Many of us, and women in particular, are brought up to be quiet, polite and reserved. We are taught that it is rude to contradict or insist on anything. As a result people sometimes repress themselves to a great degree in all their relationships. They find it impossible to state what they want to for fear of offending or being rude, but at the same time they inwardly resent the constraints upon them, and become more angry and maybe bitter as a result. Sometimes people develop very devious or manipulative forms of behaviour to try and achieve what they want. On other occasions they may restrain themselves for much of the time, but when their patience finally gives way they become demanding, aggressive or tearful, and cannot express themselves in a helpful way.

Assertiveness training is a form of therapy that aims to help people express themselves in a straightforward way, without being over-emotional or aggressive. It also demonstrates the value of persistence and negotiation. It can help one get by in many life situations where conflict arises – a mistake in a shop, returning faulty goods, explaining yourself to the doctor – situations where women in particular are often brow-beaten or patronised. In particular it can help you in close personal relationships, maybe with your children, and certainly with your ex-partner, to a constructive end.

On questioning people about whether they felt that they might benefit from assertiveness training the replies from the men were unanimous: they did not need it!

'I don't think I need it really. I can get my point across if I need to.'

'Not really. I don't think it would help me. It's only confidence.'

'I can say what I mean now. If I've got anything to say I'll say it there and then. I don't care who I hurt.'

There is no doubt that the present generation of men have generally speaking been reared to state what they want, and to persist and have confidence in their demands. Nevertheless I am sure they could benefit from some training in negotiating, expressing their feelings and in changing their opinions with grace.

The responses from the women were mixed. There were those who had never heard of assertiveness training but were quite impressed by the idea:

> 'I'm too soft. It was always put into us as children that it was rude to answer back, and that's how I am. I envy women who can be like that – not to be rude or nasty but to speak plainly. I wouldn't want to hurt people's feelings.'

There were those who had done it and found it beneficial to varying degrees:

> 'I did do some assertiveness training at the Citizens' Advice Bureau and it did help me. I think it would be useful for others too.'

> 'I have done it and I think it is helpful, but I resort to aggression. If I haven't been able to communicate I've ended up being quite aggressive.'

And there are those who do not feel that they would benefit, or who feel that they have probably developed the art of assertiveness through experience:

> 'I think it would be a marvellous idea for most people, but I suppose that I've had to teach myself to be assertive. The only thing I feel it would be useful for now is at times like job interviews. I'm very bad at selling myself although I'm not normally beaten down.'

One of the men did have some fairly reflective thoughts on how he related to his partners, indicating that he too has adapted his behaviour and perhaps gained in positive assertiveness in recent years:

'Another thing I think I might have got wrong about our marriage was that I would never argue. We never had an argument all the time we were together. I sometimes think if we had argued it might have been better. I always thought I should be man enough to give in to her. If it came to the point where there was a difference of opinion, she had her way. I don't actually argue with my girlfriend, but we discuss things. We sometimes agree to differ, but we never actually argue.'

There is no doubt that some people do develop skills of assertiveness through life experience, but others will never improve their relationship skills without some help and guidance. If you would like to try assertiveness training ask at the local library, adult education centre or Citizens' Advice Bureau whether there are any classes locally. You will have nothing to lose and you could have much to gain.

10 Sources of Help

GINGERBREAD

Gingerbread is *the* organisation for the one-parent family. They are a national charity with headquarters in London, but they have branches nationwide. National Gingerbread co-ordinates and supports over 350 groups, provides information and training for its members, and draws attention to the special needs and problems of one-parent families. Local groups are run by lone parents, for lone parents and their children. The basic aim of all groups is to increase the self-confidence of their members to enable them to face up to their situation and life in general. Members gain strength from sharing common experiences, and often develop new skills by participating and helping with Gingerbread activities.

Local groups meet regularly and, having taken the plunge often a difficult thing to do, the new member will discover that Gingerbread can do much to benefit him/her. Everybody involved is, or has been, a single parent, acutely aware of the difficulties and problems which arise from this. There may be regular advice sessions, or members may have organised a help-line so that there is always someone to phone if you need help. Everyone is also aware of babysitting problems and will try to help out. Much comfort and support is derived from casual chatting to other members in a similar situation to your own. This may always be done informally, or some groups may structure the meeting so that people can share their experiences and gain from that. Either way, the emphasis is on constructive, positive thinking, and sometimes on practical help. If those running the group cannot help you themselves, then they will know of somebody who can.

After the initial shyness and embarrassment has worn off most people are able to allow their circumstances to fall into perspective. There are bound to be occasions when something happens and help or advice is sought once more, but for some of the time members can let problems fade into the background and enjoy the other activities and events provided by the group. Another advantage of all being in the same position is that members might feel that they have 'permission' to enjoy themselves. Being a one-parent family can sometimes be similar to being bereaved, and indeed will occasionally be the result of such. For some time it can seem almost immoral to smile or laugh, but with others in the same position it can be much easier, and can start you on the road to recovering your sense of humour. One of the groups I attended organised a whole range of activities including coffee mornings, pub nights, parties, dances and outings.

Children's events feature, especially in the school holidays, when every parent is more than aware of the twin enemies – boredom and lack of money. As it says in one of their handouts:

> 'During school holidays we aim to have outings and activities for and with the children. Things that families normally do together and which we find are so much more fun to do with others, like going to the zoo, the seaside and picnics.'

Taking your children out and about on your own can be lonely and stressful. As always the responsibility for everything falls on you alone. Going in a group from Gingerbread can take away much of the worry of outings, gives you the benefit of other adults to talk to, and your children the benefit of mixing with others. You and your children will find it easier to be good-humoured and to enjoy the event more than if you were alone, and it is lovely to have others there when your youngster does that funny thing that you would like to share.

160

Gingerbread also organise group summer holidays – occasions which, as we shall see later, can be very stressful to cope with single-handed. One woman I spoke to felt that as she was older than usual when she had her children she would not fit in with the normal Gingerbread meetings, but was prepared to try a holiday with them. She found them very good and went on two occasions. She felt that if you are open-minded and do not expect too much then you will be well satisfied.

Gingerbread helps people recover from the trauma of the early days of separation and in so doing it equips them to face the future. Members are encouraged to re-invest their new-found skills to keep the group going and help others to gain the same benefits as themselves. Newcomers are welcome to attend all functions for six weeks before deciding whether or not to join the group. Members pay a small fee and receive information every three months on forthcoming events.

Contact National Gingerbread at 35 Wellington Street, London WC2E 7BN (telephone: 01 240 0953). Phone them to find out where your nearest group is.

SOLICITORS

People came by their solicitors in a variety of ways. They may have used them previously for conveyancing, or perhaps been recommended by a friend. Opinions varied as to their helpfulness or otherwise. Some people were just so grateful to be able to tell somebody how awful their lives had been that this influenced their feelings towards their solicitor. They looked upon them as social workers, marriage guidance counsellors and father confessors all rolled into one. One solicitor told me how people often ask her whether she thinks that they should get divorced or not! Other people reported what a poor service they had received – they had constantly had to phone, write and generally badger their solicitors before anything was done.

In the past, solicitors have had a reputation for making things worse between partners. When hearing the story from only one point of view it is easy for the solicitor to take your side. It can happen that this sympathetic ear adds fuel to your own indignation at what you have had to survive, and leads you to become far more aggressive and demanding than you had intended or than is helpful. Nowadays solicitors are advised to take a conciliatory tone whenever possible, especially where children are involved. A good solicitor should simply oil the wheels of separation so that there are as few bumps and bangs along the way as possible, rather than add fuel to an already potentially explosive situation.

Citizens' Advice Bureaux can direct you to solicitors who deal with marital matters, but cannot recommend them and may not know if they are particularly good. Gingerbread cannot recommend solicitors but if you join a group you will probably hear of local ones which people have used and liked. Other sources of legal advice are the National Council for One-Parent Family's help-line (*see* later), or you may be able to have a free consultation at your local Citizens' Advice Bureau. One person found a very good solicitor through 'Women's Aid' and people often commented that they preferred a woman solicitor.

When consulting a solicitor, remember that they are there to act upon your instructions. Of course, they must advise you of the law and make certain recommendations, but often people are far too easily influenced by their solicitors because they feel that they must do as they are told, which may not be what they want at all. Remember that it is you and not the solicitor who has to live with the consequences of any decisions. Do not be afraid to state your honest opinions and to re-state them if necessary. If you are striving to keep your separation or child-care arrangements as trouble-free as possible, ask to see letters before they are sent, and insist that the tone is kept business-like but unthreatening. They are writing to your ex-partner, not another lawyer. Remember that you are the customer in this relationship. The solicitor is being paid for his services and you must be in control of how things proceed.

DOCTORS

Some people found their doctors easy to approach and talk to, others found them no help. For those that were able to talk to the doctor, s/he would be prepared to listen but in all but one case made no suggestions of practical help, only prescribed drugs. In one case the woman was referred for counselling which she found very beneficial. If you want help from your doctor it is up to you to keep communicating with him or her. If you feel you need help from counselling, say so. The suggestion probably will not come from them. Let them know of your circumstances early on. Although not their direct concern it does help them understand you and the children better.

RELIGION

At one time priests and vicars would have been approached by most people thinking of divorce. These days religion is given a very low priority in these circumstances. No one I spoke to had approached their church ministers. One or two felt that they gained support from the church while their children were little, but it was more a sympathy for the children than a support for themselves. A few people admitted praying at home which they did find helpful. If you find that your circumstances drive you to prayer although it is normally foreign to you, relax and draw strength from sharing your experience with 'something' else. Do not let inhibition stop you reaching out for something which, however intangible, might well help you through a bad time.

SOCIAL WORKERS

There is a terrific barrier around social workers in terms of status and power that prevents many from approaching them. Social work is an extremely difficult job to do and there is no doubt that social workers vary considerably from one to another. If you want to approach Social Services for any of the reasons touched upon in the book, but cannot find the courage to go alone, take someone with you. Make a list before you go of what you want to say and the object of your visit. Be clear in your own mind what help you are hoping to gain from your visit. If you simply pour out all your circumstances with no apparent purpose in mind the social worker may try to help in areas that you did not intend, but fail to do so in those matters that you most need it.

CITIZENS' ADVICE BUREAU

This is an excellent organisation that can give you up to date help and information on a whole range of issues. It will often be the first port of call before being directed elsewhere. If a CAB cannot help, it will know someone who can. Find out where your nearest branch is from the phone book or library and make a note of the opening hours. Sometimes there will be long queues, but at other times the waiting will be minimal. Most bureaux have a solicitor in attendance perhaps one night a week to help with legal queries.

NATIONAL COUNCIL FOR ONE-PARENT FAMILIES

This is an organisation aiming to offer help and advice to individual parents, to publicise issues surrounding single parenthood, and to campaign for better services and support for them. They do not have local branches, but are most useful to obtain literature on local resources, for lists of interesting and helpful books, and for free, confidential advice on the law, pregnancy counselling, housing, social security, taxation and maintenance. The telephone advice line operates between 9.15 a.m. and 5.15 p.m. on Monday, Tuesday, Thursday and Friday. The address is 255 Kentish Town Road, London NW5 2LX (telephone: 01 267 1361).

DEPARTMENTS OF HEALTH AND SOCIAL SECURITY

Experiences vary once again, but in general I sense that workers in these offices try to be more helpful than they may have been in the past, when they had a reputation for prying and being judgemental. I spoke to a local officer and he stressed that one-parent families are dealt with in a matter-of-fact way, with the facts as given accepted at face value. They try to get maintenance matters sorted out as quickly as possible, trying to get a voluntary agreement pending any court action. In a small proportion of cases they may take court action themselves when a partner defaults on maintenance payments leading to a claim on the state.

As far as the lone parent is concerned, you are just another client. You can make an appointment rather than just turning up and waiting, and you should say if you have small children to try and occupy. If you cannot get out because of your children, ask for a home visit. After the initial interview much of the business is done by post. Try to be as helpful as you can, giving correct and accurate details, and after the initial strain of getting things sorted out you should receive regular payments without any trouble.

FAMILY CONCILIATION SERVICES

The first Conciliation Centre opened in Bristol in the mid-1970s, and others have since sprung up around the country. They aim to help separating families negotiate their own solutions so that the situation is made as painless as possible. You may be asked to make a contribution towards costs, but your circumstances will be taken into account, and you may pay nothing if you are entitled to legal aid. Ask at the Citizens' Advice Bureau if there is a service near you, or look in the community pages of your telephone directory.

11 A Word from the Children

It seems only fitting and most appropriate to conclude a book on this subject with a word from those who, through no fault of their own, have been brought up primarily by one parent. There is no way that I can represent all the children, or all the different outcomes, and it did not seem fair to approach younger children still totally subjected to the living arrangements of their parents. I therefore offer this small sample of older 'children's' opinions in an attempt to demonstrate some of the long-term results of single parenthood, and to encourage parents to keep striving to make it work for their children.

CHILD ONE

This 'child' is now seventeen years old and has lived with his mum and sister, three years older, since his dad moved out when he was quite young. He has seen his dad regularly over the years, although circumstances have varied, so that sometimes he was seeing him far more than others. He now stops overnight with his dad one night a week and gets on well with him.

How old were you when your parents separated?

About five years old.

Do you know why they separated?

Well, my dad worked a lot abroad. He was away a lot anyway. I don't know the actual details. I do remember some arguments. I remember making a model with my dad and him throwing it in the air and walking out. That's about the only incident I remember. I don't think I was aware that they were separated at first. Eventually my mum said that he'd got someone else. He moved abroad and he used to write me letters and I'd write back. To start with he used to come round quite often, from what I can remember.

Do you remember any effects on you at all?

Later on, when I was playing football and that sort of stuff, I used to wish he was around a bit more, but when I was younger it didn't register really.

How did it affect your sister?

It affected her more than me I think. I don't remember, but I've been told that she used to cry through the night, and have bad dreams. She doesn't see him very often now. I go and stay every weekend but she doesn't.

Did you mind people knowing?

When I was very small there didn't seem anything wrong to me really. If I'd have been older I might have understood what was happening, but being so young, I didn't really notice.

What about at school? Were there any upsetting incidents or remarks?

I don't think so. It didn't really bother me. I used to see my dad regularly, and if there was a Parents' Evening or something he would probably be there anyway, so it didn't notice.

What about when he lived abroad?

Well, he lived abroad for about three to four years but his business was based nearby, so I'd see him about once or twice a fortnight. As I got older I used to phone him, and we'd write to each other.

What happened about your grandparents, aunts and cousins on your dad's side?

I got on really well with my grandma, my dad's mum, until she died a couple of years ago. When my dad first left I used to stay for weekends with my dad's brother – my uncle and aunt. I saw more of them I think. He was more of a father figure at that time I think. He hasn't children of his own. He'd sit up playing cards with me and things. My auntie would really spoil me and make a fuss of me. I still see them quite a lot. They live quite near to my dad now.

What differences has it made, your mum being a single parent?

Well, mum's been the one there all the time to push me into things or whatever, get me to do my homework and so on, whereas I'd just see my dad. My mum was the one I'd shout at when I had a mood on. My dad's just getting a bit of that now. I see a lot more of him now. I remember asking him and nagging him – 'why aren't you here?' or 'why don't you come to see me?', and I think it used to upset him, that he couldn't be around all the time.

Were you aware of any problems that it created for your mum?

She made sure that I was not aware that she was struggling, if she was. I got everything. I never went without. We always had a holiday and that sort of thing. I think she's been determined that it would not affect us. No, I didn't notice the absence of my dad on holiday particularly. I was too busy enjoying myself!

Does it affect you in any way now?

No, not at all.

169

How would you describe your relationship with your dad now?

Very good indeed. We get on really well.

What about with your mum?

Same. I get on well with my mum. I wouldn't say my mum knows me better than my dad but she can read me more than my dad. There are probably things I'd tell my mum and not my dad and vice-versa. I do relate to them in different ways. Mum's there all the time. Dad can opt out sometimes.

Have you ever tried to play one off against the other?

I don't think so. There were times when my mum might say 'if you don't tidy your bedroom up you can go' and I'd think 'right then, I'll go, my dad doesn't live far away'. One time I stayed away for a few days and then I came back. That was because she gave me an ultimatum, and because I'd got somewhere to go.

Did you feel safe doing that?

No. I felt really bad about it.

Have either of your parents found a new partner?

Yes. My dad has. I don't mind that. If my parents have separated, then there's no reason why he shouldn't find someone else. I get on well with her. She's a bit like a mother really. When I'm round there she'll tell me off. I don't resent it. I can pull her leg. They've been together about ten years. I suppose I did resent her at the start. I'd argue with myself – if he wanted her, it was up to him, and then, well, why wouldn't he stay with us? As you get older though, you understand it more. I do.

Are there any children on her side?

No, but there's a lot of other family. They all accept me. I go to all the Christmas parties with them and so on. Her nephew is on the same course as me and we get on really well, like a real cousin. My sister doesn't have anything to do with that.

Can you say why your sister feels differently?

It's just that she's always thought, well, that's the end of him then. Very occasionally she goes round and sees him, but she never calls him dad. She just disregards him. I don't think she's really ever forgiven him, and she thinks she can do without him. I think she has grown to understand as she's got older, but she's too strong-willed to change her mind. I think she may be trying to prove her point.

Would you have preferred your mum and dad to have stayed together? Would it have been better for you if they had?

I'd say 'yes'. But the thing is, if ever there's a function or anything my mum and dad attend together. I don't know how they feel about each other, but they get on really well.

How does your mum get on with your dad's new partner?

I wouldn't say she gets on with her.

How does your dad cope with that?

He avoids it. I don't think there are many situations where they would both be there. I don't know what would happen if they were.

How would you feel if your mum were to find a new partner?

It wouldn't bother me really. I tease her about likely candidates. I don't know how I'd really feel. Depends whether I liked him.

Do you think your parents have over-indulged you?

I think my dad used to spoil me with presents, but he's

stopping that now. My mum has never been physically strict with me. She shouts, but apart from once or twice would not smack me. I don't know if I'll turn out the worse for that. I wasn't strictly disciplined, and there were times when I felt I didn't care, but I've come round in the end.

Do you think in some ways you are better off?

Well, the thing is, I don't know if I'd have such a good relationship with my dad if he'd been here all the time. He might have been hard on me. As it is he lets me make my own decisions, but we get on well.

CHILD TWO

Child number two is an only child whose parents separated when she was about thirteen. They lived 'separately' in the marital home for some considerable time before the father finally moved out. The 'child' is now eighteen years old and enjoys a good relationship with both her parents.

How old were you when your parents separated?

I was about twelve or thirteen. I first realised that something was happening when I heard my mum coming out of the spare room early in the mornings. She didn't want me to know at first, but I would hear her coming out of the little bedroom, and I could tell the bed was being slept in. I asked my mum one morning – I think it might have been Christmas morning that I asked her – and she said she didn't want me to know at that stage, because it might upset me. In a way that upset me. I felt that I was being shut out; that they didn't want me to know what was going on. I can't remember how long that went on for. It's not very clear in my memory any more.

Do you think you would have felt better if they had explained it to you first?

My mum did ask me at one stage how I'd feel if they did divorce. Well, at the time they had these times when they didn't speak, and you could cut the atmosphere with a knife, and that was the only thing that I didn't like about them still being together. That did upset me. It upset me in that half the time I didn't know what was going on. Mum never tried to keep anything from me. If I wanted to know anything, I'd go up to her and ask, and she'd tell me.

Do you know why they separated?

Well, yes and no. I've heard what my mum's said. I've never really asked my dad, because you get close to him in a different sort of way. I wouldn't dream of asking him anything like that.

How did if affect you when they actually split up?

Most people didn't know for absolutely ages because I didn't want people to talk. I didn't feel embarrassed but I was worried that everybody was going to look at me, thinking 'I wonder what's been going on in their house'? It did really upset me for ages. At school I used to try to keep it quiet and then when people found out they used to come up and say 'sorry to hear about your mum and dad' and I didn't want that in a way.

Did you tell anybody at school?

There was only one person who knew. She stopped here one night. Our cat was dying of feline leukaemia, and she'd got out. I was very upset in case she didn't come home again. I was crying in my bedroom and my mum was comforting me, and my dad came up and said: 'listen Jane, there's things going to happen in the next year that are going to upset you more.' I hadn't been told then that they were going to get divorced. Mum had only asked me how I'd feel if they did, but it was from that comment that I just gathered. That upset me more. I thought well, if it's going to be worse than this then I don't want it to happen. It wasn't in the end, because anything I wanted to know I'd ask my mum, and she never, ever tried to turn me away from my dad. Even though she had feelings against my dad, she never once tried to turn me against him. That was good in a way, because I think if she had done I don't think I would have been close to her or him now.

In what other ways did it affect you?

To get away from it all I'd go up the farm and sit with the horses for ages. And it affected me in that I'd come home, do my home-work, and when my dad came in I'd go out, because of the atmosphere really. A lot of the time I was in the middle of it, like when my mum got locked out or whatever, I was the one who had to keep getting up and letting her in. That's what affected me, when I was in the middle of it. I felt it was wrong that I felt I should have to go out of my own house all the time, but I did, because even upstairs you could tell when they were like that. The dog was really fit then, because I used to get up every night and give her a walk, and go and sit with the horses. I'd just sit there for ages watching. It's so quiet up there, you just feel you can get away from things. I used to be on my own a lot at the time.

When did you start to tell people?

I only confided in the one person at first and only because she was at my house when my Dad made that comment. Mostly people found out through a neighbour's daughter. I was mostly in the top sets at school, and a lot of those people are very 'proper'. Divorce was looked down on in a way. There was only one other person in the same position, and her parents had split up when she was little, and she has a step-father whom she regards as a dad anyway. But, then again, when I went away on a residential course recently there were five of us chatting together, and four out of the five had divorced parents – that really shocked me.

Did you mind people knowing?

I did to some extent to start with, but then I thought, well, it's no reflection on me, and once I'd come to terms with it I found it a lot easier to talk about. One thing I didn't like was talking to the social worker (to assist in the decision of who should have custody). In a way I felt that when I was talking to him, from what I said he was deciding whether I liked my mum or my dad better, and who I should live with. I didn't like that at all, so a lot of the time I didn't answer him. I only saw him once, and I didn't like it. I felt the way that he was asking questions made my mum out to be a really bad mother – things like 'oh, so your mother doesn't make your tea every night?' and I thought at the time – well, she shouldn't have to, but I didn't say that. He said at the start that if there was anything I didn't want to answer I needn't, so I'd either say 'I don't know', or 'I haven't really thought about it' – [smiles] I was really helpful.

Were any teachers involved or helpful?

Only the once. About two years ago. I happened to mention to one of the teachers that my dad lived at X. The teacher lives in X too, and I started talking to him. He was really nice. He said: 'you must have kept that really well. I'd never heard that your parents were divorced'. After that the RE teacher came up and said how shocked and sorry he was, and that was about two or three years after it. But they were really nice. I felt I could talk really openly with the first teacher. He was really nice. He wasn't any of my subject teachers, so that made it easier. He asked me questions, and I felt I could talk to him. And he said if I

175

ever got depressed or whatever to go to him. I wouldn't though. I'd probably go to one of my friend's mum, but I thought it was nice of him.

How has it happened that you confide in your friend's mum?

Well, there are two friends who I tell most things to. I haven't really got a best friend because I've got a lot of friends who I see on different nights. So I confide in those two friends, and M's mum. I've known her for years, and have seen a lot of her. And M has had some trouble with her dad in the past – not the same situation by any stretch, but it's probably what's brought us closer together. Her mum mostly just listens. She won't give you advice unless you ask for it. She doesn't try to interfere.

Were there ever any incidents or remarks at school that upset you?

Only once. Just before the divorce, we'd all been to a wedding reception, and the girl from over the road was there. My dad showed my mum up on the dance floor. He either abused another man or said something to my mum, but my mum went home straight away. At school a lot of people knew about it, and I hadn't even told those I do confide in. It had got round the class and people were coming up to me and asking about it. I don't like being pushed into telling things. I like to do it in my own time. I felt they were trying to find out what was going on. That upset me. I don't think that there were any other children in the class that had divorced parents.

What happened about your grandparents, aunts and cousins on your dad's side?

That hasn't changed really. The only time it made it awkward was when my mum and I would visit my nan together. My dad was living there for a time, and if he should come in while we were there it made it difficult for my nan, because she'd obviously stick up for her own son, but she still really liked my mum. There was nothing else really.

Can you think of any ways in which you've been affected by living with only one parent?

I still don't think of me as being in a one-parent family. My dad comes round when he can in the week, usually two or three times. He's said to me that I can go over to his place any time, just to let him know. So I see my dad, and my mum's always here, so I don't think of it as a one-parent family.

How has your relationship with your dad been affected?

I've got closer to him, in a different way to my mum. Now I can talk to either of them about most things. I've got closer to my dad probably because I don't see him so much. When we do see each other we get on well. We've got more to say to each other. At one time I felt that he didn't visit me enough. I was really pleased with an event that I'd done well in, and I came running down the lane to tell him. He just said 'well done, Bab,' and that was it. I couldn't believe it really. I thought he could have said something else. I didn't tell him. I just got really upset. I started ignoring him. And when he came round, he wouldn't say 'hello' straight away he'd play with the dog. I got upset and I said 'God, you only come to see the dog anyway,' and I marched upstairs. My mum talked to me and she said that by ignoring him I was treating him the way he used to treat her, and she said 'you're like your dad in a lot of ways, but you're going to push him away, and you'll make him more reluctant to come over and see you if every time he comes over you're like that with him', which really made me think. She said: 'If you're going to be funny with him, say why you feel like that. Have it out with him.' So now I do tend to do that and he does respond. You might have to repeat it about three times, but he does. It's made it better now. I've had to try hard. Once you've got over that barrier of the first step – I thought 'I can't do this, I can't just come out and say "look Dad",' but once you start doing it it's easier. He then knows and respects how you feel, and he can change then. So once you've got over that it's a lot easier.

Do you think it would have been harder if you had been younger?

No, I think it would have been easier. When you're little everything just passes you by. Nothing's real. Your early teens are the worst. That's the time you've got to make decisions, about your life, your options at school, and if you've got a lot of other things on your mind it tends to cram your mind and you can't concentrate.

Have either of your parents found a new partner?

Yes, my dad. He lives with Penny. She's forty and she's got two sons of her own. They don't live there any more. They got kicked out. I think they live with their aunt and their nan. One's nearly eighteen and the other's fifteen. I don't pry too much in that side of my dad's life, because they got on well, and I got on well with the lads. But I think I'd have found it harder if they had been girls. It didn't bother me when I found out they were two boys, because I wasn't threatened. I was still his only daughter. I think it might have been different if Penny had had a daughter. I think it would have been harder too if they had been younger. It was good that they were about my age, and also, they were worse off than me because they haven't really seen their dad since they were under five. I've still got both my parents and I still see both of them, but they've only got their mum. I never felt jealous when my dad gave them attention.

How did you feel towards your dad's partner?

When I first met her I took a friend, so that I'd got someone to fall back on – so that if the conversation stopped – well, my friend just talks anyway! I felt at first that she got on better with my friend. I felt a bit put out at first. But I talked to my friend about it and realized that she probably had to try harder with me, because in a way she probably feels that I come between her and my dad, and in a way I feel that she comes between my dad and me. She's really nice. I didn't dislike her at all. She's really friendly. I called in last week not realising that my dad wouldn't be there, and I didn't feel uncomfortable with her at all.

How do you think you would feel if your mum had a new partner?

I'd be really happy for her. She did go out with someone in the beginning, for about eighteen months, and I did mind at first. But I thought well she can't just stop living. And when I got used to the idea, I'd got no objections. I might feel differently if they were to move in and live here, because that would restrict the freedom that I've had for so long. I'd really try, because I wouldn't want to make my mum's life unhappy, but I'd have to try hard, I really would. At present I'm really messy. I can tell my mum what time I want to come in, so long as I stick to it. But if someone else lived here you'd have to consider them as well, not just your mum. There'd have to be more give and take, because of this other person. I'd really try though, because I don't like to see my mum unhappy. When she gets depressed I don't know what to say to her. I don't know how she's feeling – she tries to tell me, but I can't say I understand because I've never gone through those situations. I can tell just the way she opens the door what kind of mood she's in, and that does affect me in a lot of ways. Sometimes I'm silly, for instance running around with the dog and making a lot of noise just to annoy mum, but you have to tread carefully with her sometimes.

Do you think that you've grown up a lot quicker than you would have?

Yes, but I don't mind really. Because I mean, I haven't really grown up yet. I'm learning something new every day.

Would you have preferred your mum and dad to have stayed together? Do you think it would have been better for you if they had?

If they had been happy, yes. Definitely. But the way it was, I'd have hated it even more, because if they'd stayed together, that situation would have been going on now another five years, and I couldn't have taken that. I think I'd have worn the dog out by now! I think they did the right thing. I'm really pleased that they get on now too. At first my dad used to come round, but he wouldn't come in if he knew my mum was in, and he'd just grunt. But she never gave in, for my sake really. She'd always say 'would you like a cup of tea' and he'd just grunt, so she'd have to ask me, 'does your dad want a cup of tea'. It was really hard after he first moved out, but my mum never gave up on him. She'd always be friendly and polite though she knew damn well he wouldn't reply. But she never gave in, and in the end he started to come round. I think it was a lot to do with Penny. When he started a relationship with her the situation got getter between my mum and dad. I'm really thankful for Penny in that way. Now if my dad comes round to see me and I'm not here, he'll sit and have a cup of tea with my mum. That pleases me. Their separation doesn't bother me now, as long as they speak and can be civil with each other when I'm not there, its worked out well.

Are there any situations now where it still embarrasses you or makes you feel uncomfortable?

The main thing is when you meet someone new. You don't tell them your whole life-story in the first ten minutes, but as they get to know you. Most of my friends I've known either since the primary school, or the beginning of the secondary school, so they have seen me go through all that. When you meet new people and start to get to know them, it is embarrassing in a lot of ways, because they want to know. They want to know about you and they keep asking questions. I look at other people and wonder what to say. But then I've a friend whose father used to drink and take it out on her mum, and she still doesn't talk to her dad if she can help it, which makes me realize how lucky I am. Her mum won't let the dad anywhere near the house, if he comes round he has to stand outside. I'd hate that. That would have affected me even worse. I'm glad the way it's worked out. It's a pity they had to divorce, but it's worked out well when I compare myself with other people.

Do you think your friend suffers a lot from her parents' antagonism to each other?

Yes, because I can't ever imagine hating my dad, like she hates hers. She says she hates him. I don't think she does at all. I think its mainly influences, because her brothers don't like him. Her attitude comes from home. She's influenced by her mother.

CHILD THREE

In this case the 'child' is now thirty years old and looks back to her childhood, when she was brought up exclusively by her mother from the age of about six. She had a brother who was two years younger than her, and two half-sisters from a previous marriage who lived elsewhere.

How old were you when your parents separated?

Quite honestly I can't remember exactly. I can't remember the day it happened, although I do recall lots of incidents that led up to it. I remember lots of fights, and lots of aggression once I'd gone to bed. Lots of tears from my mother. I can remember my father not being around an awful lot, but I can't really remember the time when he wasn't there at all. It sort of all blends into one. I must have started school because I remember the occasion when my mother was obviously finding it a struggle to manage and I was told: 'You are going to have free dinners at school'. I thought: I'll never manage three dinners!' It didn't bother me at that age, although it did later on. I don't think I felt different at all really.

Do you know why they separated?

Well, no. It's never ever been explained to me. I would say that my mother's a difficult woman to get on with. She's been married and divorced twice. So I don't know really why they split up.

Do you remember whether it affected your brother?

No, not at all. I can't remember it affecting my brother at all. He can probably remember things even less than I can.

Did you ever mind people knowing about it?

I did later on. In those days there was far more of a stigma, at least I felt that there was.

How did you explain your situation to people?

I can't remember anybody asking me that. I remember worrying about what I would say if they did ask me, or in case they asked me where my father was.

Did you know where your father was?

No. But it wasn't until I was much older that I became curious about where he was. I can't understand that now. I look back and think 'why wasn't I curious about where he was?'. But because he wasn't supporting us – he had various heart attacks, and I don't suppose he was working regularly – because of that my mother would never allow him to see us. I can remember when I was about eight or nine she showed me a letter that was from my father and he was asking to see the children. She wouldn't let him see us.

Why would she not allow him to see you?

Because she felt bitter about being left I suppose, and because he wasn't keeping us financially. I remember stopping myself saying 'oh, please, can't I go and see him,' because I knew it would hurt her feelings. Even at that age I thought 'I'd love to go and see my father'. I did want to go and see my father, and I don't feel any bitterness at all towards this man that had left us, more bitterness towards this woman who was preventing us from seeing him.

What happened to your father subsequently?

My father died when I was twelve. Just as I was reaching the age when I could have possibly got on a train and gone to see him, which was my intention all along – one day I'll see my father. My mother told me of my father's death. I was surprised that she was quite upset at the time. I was amazed that she was. She never had any feeling for anyone really, but she was upset. I thought: 'well, why is she so upset? She hated this man'. I suppose it was a part of life that had suddenly come to an end. I was very upset, just at the time I was beginning to feel my feet and think I might see him. But, it was easier then to explain, to say that my father was dead.

Do you remember any incidents or remarks at school that upset you?

The only time it caused any embarrassment, really, was when there were letters going out to parents, and they were always addressed to fathers. My mother is not the sort of woman to have the education, intelligence or that sort of thought in her head to think that the child might be in

183

difficulty at school, or to explain, and of course twenty years ago I don't think there were so many people divorced. I don't think my mother ever came up to school to explain anything. She wouldn't have been able to explain it to me, let alone to the teachers. I don't think it would cross her mind that we might be having trouble. She was having trouble, nobody else. I can remember getting embarrassed when they got round to subjects like parents, and fathers, and what did they do for a living. My friends knew there was no man at my house, but I think they just accepted it as well. We were so small when it happened. But I can remember an incident at the senior school when a teacher asked me where my father's family was from, and I had to say that I really didn't know. That was really embarrassing. He was saying: 'why don't you know?' It was really stupid of the teacher to have pressed that. Very embarrassing in adolescence.

What happened about your grandparents, aunts or cousins on your dad's side?

Well, I've never seen them, as far as I know. I've never seen any of my grandparents anyway. I think they were all dead before I was born. I've never been in touch with any relatives on my father's side, and if ever I mention it to my mother she doesn't want to know.

Would you like to track them down now?

Yes, I would. Particularly when I was younger I wanted to. I suppose that I would. I would very much. But I don't know if I could cope with their reaction if they didn't want to know. But then I don't feel that I was rejected by my father. I don't feel that at all. I think he might have been driven away! But I don't feel that he deserted us, or that he's a bad man at all. I would have liked the chance to have known him better.

Was your mum a single parent for long? In what ways were you affected?

Yes. She hasn't remarried since, although she's had various boyfriends. We were very badly off. I never ever had new clothes. I had everything second-hand, shoes, everything. I went on holiday with the next door neighbours once. But then, I didn't feel different from anybody else. I don't think in those days people did take their kids out like they do today. I didn't feel deprived. We were poor, but we weren't rough. We were clean and presentable. The only way I felt affected was that at times my mum would work day and night. She would work in a factory in the day and in a pub at night. When I was seven I would look after my brother at night. I remember that very clearly, and I remember being upset at that, thinking I don't like being left on my own. That was horrible. Other times when she couldn't work because she was ill or worn out we would go back on social security.

Does it affect you now in any way?

I don't think it does. I don't know whether if I'd had a father there all the time it would have made me any different, or better or anything else. I'm very aware of children who have far more, financially, and of people who were allowed an education. I had to start work, not only to help provide for the rest of the family, but because I was so sick and tired of having second-hand everything. I wanted to get out there and do something to make me feel more normal.

And did you feel better after you started work?

Yes, I suppose I did. I was reliant upon myself then, rather than having to rely on anyone else.

Looking back, do you think your mum had any problems disciplining you?

I don't think so with me. I think my brother may have been a bit difficult. He's a bit of a tearaway. Definitely a bit of a tearaway. But I wasn't. I was always aware of being good, because my mother had problems enough. So I was always very well-behaved, perhaps too much.

Did either of your parents find a new partner?

No. My dad didn't have any other partner. It was just a matter of having enough of my mother. They had lived together for six years before they got married. Then they got married and had all this trouble. I think my mother expects too much of people. I think she thought when they married that he'd change into a Prince Charming, and a good provider. I think when they lived together she probably accepted him but thought that if they got married he'd change. My mum did have one serious boyfriend when I was between the ages of ten and fourteen. I didn't like him. I didn't like him at all. I don't think I was jealous of him, but I don't think she was ever very fond of him. If she had been fond of him and he of her, and they had been genuinely happy then I think I would have been happy, but they weren't. He couldn't have cared less really, and mother couldn't have cared less. It was just somebody to spend time with. She used to like ballroom dancing and I think they were good partners. I think it would have been nice if they had been genuinely fond of each other. It would have been nice for her to meet someone, I would have appreciated that. It was upsetting because she was spending a lot of time with a man who was a waste of space really.

Would you have preferred your parents to have stayed together? Do you think it would have been better for you if they had?

I don't think so. I never thought 'I wish that they'd stayed together and not split up'. I never realised that they had really. I just accepted it. I think it would have been far worse if I had been older. When you are in your teens there is so much going on in your own life that you really don't want anything in the background to become more important. You want it to remain constant.

Index